HOW TO STEAL A MILLION:

The memoirs of a Russian hacker

No man is rich enough to buy back his past.

Oscar Wilde

CONTENTS

Foreword To The English Edition 1

Chapter 1 4
    KNOCKING ON HEAVEN'S DOOR

Chapter 2 10
    THE LAWYER

Chapter 3 13
    CARDING 101

Chapter 4 22
    VOLODARKA, OH VOLODARKA

Chapter 5 29
    NO FENCE AGAINST A FAIL

Chapter 6 34
    ROADS

Chapter 7 37
    DARK ELVIS

Chapter 8 40
    EVERYBODY LIES

Chapter 9 45
    TOO BIG FOR MINSK

Chapter 10 48
    A LITTLE HOLIDAY

Chapter 11 55
    TWO AND A HALF YEARS?

Chapter 12 57
    ARREST

Chapter 13 64
    BADB

Chapter 14 71
    CELLMATES

Chapter 15 74
    THE ASKING NEVER ENDS

Chapter 16 78
    A PROMISING YOUNG MAN

Chapter 17 81
    CARDERPLANET

Chapter 18 87
    LEVIAFAN

Chapter 19 90
    INNOCENT UNTIL PROVEN GUILTY

Chapter 20 94
    WHEN A FRIEND LETS YOU DOWN

Chapter 21 97
    FINDING NICRON

Chapter 22 99
    NICRON

Chapter 23 102
    IN KYIV

Chapter 24 104
    MY FIRST $100

Chapter 25 112
    VIVE LA UKRAINE!

Chapter 26 115
    RULES OF PRISON LIFE

Chapter 27 118
    DRUGS IN THE CAR

Chapter 28 120
    STEPFATHER

Chapter 29 123
    NEW YEAR PLANS

Chapter 30 126
    NEW YEAR

Chapter 31 131
    TRIAL

Chapter 32 136
    A COMPROMISE

Chapter 33 141
    DUMPSMARKET

Chapter 34 146
    LORD, PROTECT ME FROM MY FRIENDS

Chapter 35 153
    JONNYHELL

Chapter 36 156
    SENTENCING

Chapter 37 159
   THE PRICE OF FREEDOM

Chapter 38 162
   GREAT WITS BRING CASH OR TROUBLE

Chapter 39 168
   FREEDOM

Chapter 40 183
   I REMEMBER THE TIME…

Chapter 41 185
   THE TAIL

Chapter 42 191
   THE KING IS DEAD. LONG LIVE THE KING!

Chapter 43 194
   A CARDER-FIGHTER BECOMES… A CARDER

Chapter 44 197
   ADULT

Chapter 45 199
   SPAM

Chapter 46 203
   SONELAO

Chapter 47 206
   YOU HAVE THE RIGHT TO REMAIN SILENT

Chapter 48 209
   THE KGB

Chapter 49 214
   FAMILIAR TERRITORY

Chapter 50 217
    WHO IS MR. GONZALEZ?

Chapter 51 219
    GONZALEZ, SUVOROV, YASTREMSKIY

Chapter 52 223
    RIGHTS THAT MAKE YOU RIGHT

Chapter 53 225
    THERE'S A BLACK SHEEP IN EVERY FLOCK

Chapter 54 229
    PRISON NO. 8

Chapter 55 234
    TALL TALES

Chapter 56 237
    HUNGER STRIKE

Chapter 57 239
    HELPING OUR ENEMIES

Chapter 58 244
    ROGUE COPS

Chapter 59 246
    THINGS ARE MOVING, GENTLEMEN OF THE JURY!

Chapter 60 249
    PRISON IS THE EASY PART

Chapter 61 255
    WHY WORK WHEN YOU DON'T NEED TO?

Chapter 62 258
    HIGH-SECURITY PENAL COLONY

Chapter 63 261
    AFTER DINNER COMES THE RECKONING

Chapter 64 264
    FEMME FATALE

Chapter 65 268
    THEIR WAYS

Chapter 66 270
    THE CORRECTIONAL PROCESS

Chapter 67 272
    NEW YEAR, NO PHONE

Chapter 68 276
    A GOOD COP IS A DEAD COP

Chapter 69 281
    HUMAN EXHAUSTION

Epilogue 287

List of Characters 289

Acknowledgements 294

FOREWORD TO THE ENGLISH EDITION

I wrote this book in prison, much of it on a banned mobile phone. It was my survival strategy: I kept working on the book, asking for an early parole and doing everything to make sure my pleas reached the ears of those who mattered. Writing helped me stay sane, distance myself from day-to-day worries and forget the bastards with whom I was surrounded.

My wife at the time believed this book was written for her. My mother thought I'd put my story on paper because I had to keep myself busy. My best friend says I am crazy to be sharing *that* kind of information. He thinks even jail can't satiate my hunger for fame. And they're all right in their different ways. It was first published in Russian in 2013, while I was still behind bars.

I need to say straight up that title of the English edition is not completely accurate. Strictly speaking, I am neither Russian, nor a hacker.

I was born and grew up in Belarus, the country many like to refer to as the "last dictatorship in Europe." And while I dabbled in hacking, I wasn't strictly speaking a hacker — I was what is known as a carder, a cyber-lord who turned stolen credit card information into money.

But I operated in the Russian-speaking hacking world that was concentrated in Ukraine, Russia and Belarus during the first flowering of Slavic cyber-crime, and worked with some of the biggest cyber-criminals who moved easily between these three countries — so the "Russian hacker" label is not entirely inappropriate.

Before I came to the attention of the Belarusian police and the FBI, my online friends knew me as PoliceDog. For a few years I had more money than I knew what to do with. Aged 20, I was earning $100,000 a month — an unbelievable sum in Belarus in the early 2000s. I also tried my hand at spam, pornography and many other cyber-crime sidelines.

Had my friends and I had begun life in a different country and at a different time, many of us could have been bank employees, businessmen or owners of companies. Some, of course, would still have become criminals. But we were born in the Soviet Union at the turn of an epoch and we became adults in the 1990s when old moral values had been rejected and new ones hadn't yet appeared. We became cyber-criminals not because we were naturals, but because of the times: our parents were working two or three jobs to make ends meet, and we, the kids, were left on our own. No-one told us stealing was a sin, and even if they did, no one bothered to explain why. But everyone around us was stealing, from civil servants to businessmen: and almost everyone got away with it. Why couldn't we do the same? Who stopped us and showed us what was right? We spent days sitting in front of computers (they appeared first in the families of scientists, engineers, university professors) and we devoted ourselves to the first thing we discovered on the Internet. We numbed our feeling of guilt with the idea we weren't targeting anyone personally, only large companies and governments, that we were a band of merry Robin Hoods. Someone even came up with the term "economic guerillas": we steal in the West and spend at home.

Psychologically it's not hard to convince yourself that you're not doing anything wrong.

Like most, I ended up in prison, where I was lucky to spend only a decade. My beautiful wife left me. My mother aged with grief rather than time. My friends started seeing me as a ghost, someone they had nothing to talk to about. You don't share joy from your child's birthday or your summer trip with a ghost — it's too awkward.

In 2015, I was released — aged 31.

It may sound crazy, but I'm grateful for those lost years: for getting time to think and analyze my life and everything I had done before jail. I began to understand the true value of my nearest and dearest, of myself and of my life.

This book is about my time as a successful cyber-criminal and my experience in the Belarusian penal system, which has changed little since the Soviet Union. The events and people are real. The way they are depicted, however, is my own. I've changed a few names and removed some altogether. I've softened some things and embellished others — it's something all authors do. It is up to you to decide if I can be trusted. Read — and draw your own conclusions.

Moscow, April 2018

CHAPTER 1

KNOCKING ON HEAVEN'S DOOR

I guess at that moment on September 16th, 2004, my brain rescued me from the situation I found myself in. I couldn't see or hear anything around me. I didn't see the grey ceiling above me, I saw something very different instead: Dmitry is looking out of the window, Katya is silently cutting bread at the table, Fidel is telling a joke and trying to take a stuffed boar's head off the wall.

The door swings open and that cop walks in, accompanied by another four in civilian clothes… "Good evening…" That's it… I've been replaying that moment in my head over and over again, "Good evening…"

My name is Sergey Pavlovich. Online, a lot of people know me as PoliceDog, panther[757], Fallen Angel or diplomaticos.

We were in Lipen, a village 100 kilometers from Minsk. Our country house was the last one on the street. Right behind it was an endless forest with wild boars and foxes: the forest my grandfather looked after as a forester all his life. It was my girlfriend Katya's house. By then we had already moved to the capital, but we still lived a lot of the time in Lipen. God, I loved that country house.

Two things seemed strange. Firstly, why did they have to arrest me after I left Minsk and turn it into a field operation? I wasn't trying to hide. They could have come to my place in Minsk and handcuffed me. It would've been way easier. They may have wanted to arrest me while I was relaxed, drinking with friends. Then they should have acted sooner: two days earlier we had been celebrating the anniversary of DumpsMarket, my website. Serious carders had arrived from all over the former USSR. As the founder of DumpsMarket, I was the birthday boy. Alcohol was flowing like water, hookers were dancing on the tables. Had the cops attended that party, they would have been in for a nice surprise. However, they were uninterested in our criminal Sabbath. Which leads me to think that the information they had on me came very, very suddenly.

If only that police lieutenant who had stopped me for speeding knew that my phone was being tapped or that I was being watched, he might have reconsidered taking that $20. But it wasn't about him anymore. Maybe someone had said the address over the phone after all, and the task force dashed to find us. Or had they actually been following us all the way from Minsk? Oh, to hell with it! Finding out my whereabouts was probably the easiest thing the cops had to do. It's still strange, though.

Now to the guests. The heroes of my locked room detective story:

- Katya, my girlfriend.
- Dmitry Burak (Graph), we are actually cousins but I consider him my brother and my best friend. We've been through a lot. I grew up thinking of him as of my real brother, so that's what I call him. I keep no secrets from him. He's my right hand.
- Sergey Storchak, (Fidel). He came over all the way from his home in Odessa for the DumpsMarket anniversary and sort of just stayed here. I guess, he liked it. Fidel's birthday is on

September 17th. That's what we were celebrating. Fidel is a key partner. I don't trust him much, so Dmitry's the one working with him.

- Ilya Saprykin, (Postal), a clever Jewish boy. He worked with us and was informed about a lot of what was going on. Postal could have sold me out. He had more than enough information to do that... And how could I forget he arrived separately from everyone else! He broke off at the last moment, said he had stuff to do in Minsk. We left for Lipen without him. And only two hours later, when the sauna and kebabs were ready and waiting, Ilya's navy-blue BMW drove into the front yard.
- Katya, Saprykin's girlfriend.
- Kirill Kalashnikov (Kaizer), just 17 years old. He worked with us, but he lived in Yekaterinburg, Russia. He arrived in Minsk for the anniversary and, just like Fidel, decided to stay for the party in Lipen.

I remember guys taking guns and going to the back yard to shoot cans. I was a better shot than others. It was really exciting. I was jumping on tires dug into the ground around the flower beds, and falling like an idiot. I guess I was high on fresh air. Dmitry fired a shot, and I pretended to be wounded. I toddled a few meters away and fell on the ground. My fingers found the place where the bullet went in and pressed the throbbing gush of blood. I could feel my heart beat even through the jacket. Clouds were floating high in the sky. The air was so transparent in the fall, it would be a shame to die under skies that beautiful. To lie on the golden yellow leaves and slowly turn cold.

When I opened my eyes, the sky was already gone. Katya's face covered everything. Huge tender eyes. Their single look is enough to make your heart stop beating.

"Do you love me?"

No, Katya wouldn't betray me. Although she had her reasons. I cheated on her, I didn't love her, I… as if that wasn't enough! When the men in uniform came, she was the only one that remained calm. Upon hearing "Good evening!" she went up to them.

"Hello. What's the matter?"

"Police. Whose house is this?"

"My father's."

And for some reason she calmly repeated the address and her father's full name. That calmed me down. It sounded like we thought they didn't see the house number in the dark and knocked on a wrong door. As if they were actually going to the tractor driver who lived across the street or to our neighbor to buy some fresh milk. And we had neither milk nor alcohol. Have a good one, guys! But the cops weren't going to leave.

"Were you shooting? The neighbors complained about some shooting," the only officer that was wearing a uniform explained the reason of their visit. For some reason, he was holding a gun.

"We were shooting cans. With an air gun," Katya began in the same relaxed reasonable tone, but Ilya interrupted.

"I can go to my car to show you the air guns. You know we don't need a license for them, right?"

What a hysterical idiot! A kid would know you don't need a license for a stupid air gun, I bet the cops would know it too. Meanwhile, the officers seemed to grow tired of putting up a performance.

Before I could blink, one of the men in black walked up to me and handcuffed me. The others were told to remain in the room.

Dmitry looked frightened. He was sitting on the window sill and looking at me as if asking: what should we do now? I have always been the older brother, despite being three months younger.

Nah, Dmitry isn't a traitor. He'd sooner cut off his own hand. Someone has sold us both out.

The officers expressed their desire to look around. Not to search it, but to look around, because you need the prosecutor's permission for a proper search. Saprykin started swirling nervously around the room, acting like a liberal protester who was going to report oppression to the authorities. He could have been the snitch. And his behavior could have been an act. Later, he lost confidence and just sat there biting his nails. His girlfriend seemed to have more composure. Like a prostitute held by the police, she was watching everything with an air of confidence, and even a smile. Maybe, she was enjoying the show, understanding she was just a spectator. Jumping ahead, she'll have her chance to be in our shoes. Andrey Malyshev, her step father, the director of several car dealerships, will be charged with failure to pay customs taxes, flee Belarus and be put on the international wanted list.

Fidel was smoking silently. It was hard to read his mind. He might have been thinking, "What a great present from my Belarusian friends…"

Kaizer was blinking with fear. In his face you could read, "I'll tell you everything, just let me leave Belarus."

I had thought about a possible arrest umpteen times to frighten myself. It's the same as imagining your mum has died and feeling sorry for yourself. It's nice to know you can pinch yourself at any time and make the nightmare go away. But that day everything was real. And I have to admit, I was afraid. I sat down and tried to imagine that it was all just a dream but the feeling of handcuffs on my wrists brought me straight back to reality. Katya was looking at me.

"Bunny, can you hear me? Listen. We don't know what's going to happen to you. The only thing you can do now is to eat. Because when will be the next time?" Katya's eyes started to water.

That night I was almost force-fed rice with meat, kebabs and salad. Katya hid a piece of bread in my jacket pocket. I was watching her, surprised how quickly she took to the role of convict's wife.

Do you want to know what's it like to be in a pre-trial detention center for the first time?

First, you get to the holding cell. Then the general cell. Minsk pre-trial smells of sour cabbage. You won't find a smell like that at any changing room at any gym. You'll be willing to pay any money to get out of there.

I couldn't eat, couldn't sleep. At night, I was delirious instead of dreaming. Even in my dreams I was looking for a way out, I tried to wrap my head around what'd happened. What should I tell the detectives? How can I pass a note with important directions to people outside? Five days went by like that. Eventually, I exhausted myself into falling asleep. I plunged into the darkness where there was no smell of cabbage, gray walls or numb despair.

CHAPTER 2

THE LAWYER

"Have a look," a middle-aged woman I've never seen before threw a newspaper article onto the table in front of me. It was about my arrest.

"That's quite a record. What's white plastic and where did you get the PIN-codes for those cards?"

"Here we go…" I looked at her with distrust. "I don't even know you, and you start off with a bunch of questions."

"Sergey, I am not an investigator, but I'm going to ask similar questions. To protect you as well as I can, I need to have information. I understand you may not trust me now, I know all those rumors the guys in the cell have about lawyers working with the cops. She casually mentioned the biggest concern everybody in prison has when it comes to talking to lawyers.

I wasn't considering telling her everything straightaway, and she had just named the reason. I guess, it was written all over my face, because she suddenly stood up and dragged her chair closer to the light. I could finally take a good look at her. A stout woman in her late forties. She was almost old enough to be my mother. A high forehead, university professor glasses, an old-fashioned hair-do and eyes with huge pupils — because of the darkness of the room. She stared at me with those eyes without blinking, like a cobra.

"Listen, Sergey, your brother hired me. He's very worried about you."

If any words could win me over, my lawyer had just said them. I had been at the pretrial detention center for a week and didn't know anything about Dmitry. I knew they let Katya go the same day — she had nothing at all to do with all of this. But what had happened to my brother: was he interrogated, where was he taken after the police station — I didn't know any of that. For all I knew, he could be sitting in the cell next door with no idea what had happened to me…

"You mean he's alright?"

"Yes, he is. He's out of trouble. Unlike you."

Once again in my life I got the feeling that something surreal was happening. The ashtray nailed to the table, the dim light, the woman I didn't know. Where's my mum? Could she just hug me? I'd cry and say I'm sorry and they'd let me go? That worked when I was a kid. Or maybe, I can just pinch myself and wake up in my own bed? The lawyer must have sensed the way I was feeling because she continued somewhat more forcefully.

"I need to know everything! How did you get passwords to other people's credit cards?"

I slightly pinched myself under the table. Then got myself together and looked my cobra dead in the eye.

"Not so fast. May I look at your lawyer ID first?"

"Yes," she reached into her pocket and produced a tag with the number of the room we were in and a little plastic folder.

"Galina Nesterovich," I read out. "Minsk Central District Legal Aid Bureau."

"Are you sure now I'm not an undercover cop?" Galina asked with a smile.

"You can never be too sure…"

CHAPTER 3

CARDING 101

"Let me repeat the question, how did you get the passwords to other people's cards?" Galina wasn't giving up.

"What passwords? Have you any idea what a credit card is?"

"Well, I've got one…"

The lawyer tried to laugh it off, but she looked away and admitted defeat, definitely embarrassed.

"To be honest, I've no idea about all that IT stuff, I only got the card two weeks ago."

Her purse's zipper flashed, and with the rustle of some papers, Galina fished out her credit card.

"You can definitely sleep a peaceful sleep. It is a debit Visa Electron, the most ubiquitous card in Russia and Eastern Europe. You're safe with this one — carders like me hardly ever care about them."

"Which ones do you care about, then?"

"The ones that have money on them. Visa Signature, for example. I managed to take $9900 off one in one go. I think the BIN was 414750."

"That's massive! How much did you make a month?"

"Uh… About $30,000?" (I had to bite my tongue not to blurt out the real figure, $100,000)

"So, you're a carder…" Galina said, musingly.

"Yes. Credit card thieves call each other carders. And our victims are cardholders".

"And what's 'Signature'?"

"Visa Signature is a name card for very wealthy people".

"And the 'bin'?"

"BIN (that is, Bank Identification Number) is the first six digits of the card's number that will tell you the issuing bank and the card's type. All information about BINs is stored in special data bases. For example, BIN 371535 is American Express CENTURION. And if we punch 414750 (that'd be Visa Signature that I've mentioned) into the base, we'll see the following:

BIN: VISA ® 414750
Issuer: Merryl Lynch Bank USA
Issuer Phone: 800-637-7455
Country: United States
Funding Type: CREDIT
Card Type: SIGNATURE

Not only a bank can issue a card. Credit unions and even big retail chains have their own cards (discount cards, in case with the stores)."

"What is the 'funding type'? You said my Electron was a 'debit'…"

"All cards are either credit or debit. The credit ones hold the bank's money that you spend, and then give back to the bank. And the bank charges you a small interest for using their money. When you open a debit card, you've got no money in your account, and you will only be able to use the money that you put there. Your own money, that is. In ex-Soviet countries people call any bank card a credit card, but it's not exactly right."

"My husband has got some other kind of Visa, a better one, I think…"

"The one that's better than Electron is called Classic. It's a card for clients that have used bank cards before. Gold and Platinum cards are prestigious ones, they're supposed to show off their owner's money. There are Corporate cards for medium and large companies, whose employees often travel abroad on business trips. These cards make it much easier to monitor their spending. Technically, Classic, Gold, Platinum, and Corporate are basically the same cards with different design and the issue and operation costs. Sometimes you can take much more money off an American Classic than a Gold or a Platinum."

"How so?"

"I think a lot of Americans, just like Russians, go after Gold and Platinum cards to show off. Classic is quite enough for simple everyday use. However, it's much easier to pick up a girl at the bar if you casually flash your Visa Platinum. Then again, a Ferrari key will do just as fine."

"I've got a Visa, you mentioned MasterCard… Which one did you have?"

"Me?!" I was taken aback by her naivety. "None. Banks and payment systems can't provide full protection of your money on their accounts no matter how much they want to. Also, it's extremely easy to track one's purchases and travels through his card. And in my line of work it's best to remain invisible."

"It's all very interesting," the lawyer interrupted me. "But we are digressing. What are the charges against you? 'Property theft at trade and service enterprises of Minsk through fake credit card data (Visa and MasterCard credit cards) totaling $9,000, directed similar crimes, committed by Voropayev and Batyuk.' I understand all of that, but what 'false data' did you use, and how did you use it?"

"Ordinary people believe that the money is somehow 'in' the credit card itself, but that's wrong — the money isn't there physically. The card is a kind of a key to an account at the bank that issued that card. In other words, it identifies the account owner and confirms that he or she has the access to some sort of a vault in the bank, where the money is. The seller swipes the card through the POS-terminal (POS stands for the Point of Sale) — a device that reads the information from the card's magnetic stripe and contacts the bank to carry out the transaction. The bank contacts the credit card processing center and sends there the data from your credit card. Then the processing center contacts the bank that issued the card and receives a coded confirmation or decline. A successful transaction's code is 00 — APPROVED. Otherwise there's a ban on the transaction. Visa is a payment system that connects all of the above together and charges up to 3.5% of every transaction."

"I understand that. But what does it have to do with the 'fake data'?"

"Easy. The card is counterfeit, I'm not its rightful owner, therefore, any payment I make is fake by default."

"And the cashiers have no idea the card is not genuine?"

"Of course not. The dump was real, and the money was discarded off a real account. The only fake thing is the card itself that the dump was written off to."

"What's a 'dump'?"

"A dump is all the information from the credit card's magnetic stripe. It's composed of three tracks. The first two are necessary to process transactions, the third one holds technical information. The second track is the most important. The first track duplicates the main data of the second one — the card's number, expire date, CVV-code, and the cardholder's name.

> Track1:
> B4559907560784214^SMITH/JOHN^1102101000000000000000527000000
>
> Track2: 4559907560784214=11021010000052700000

The 101 after the card's expire date means that the card is international. If it's 201 instead, it means that the card is only valid in the country where it was issued. If you have track2, you can easily generate track1, but doing it the other way around is quite troublesome. Track2 is enough to get cash at an ATM."

"Where did you get the dumps?"

"There are several ways. You can make, or buy, a portable card reader that, as the name suggests, reads the information off the card's magnetic stripe. The smallest card readers I've seen were as big as a matchbox and were manufactured in Ukraine by engineers from Boa Factory. Those devices are distributed to cashiers at upscale boutiques, waiters and expensive prostitutes, and they simply swipe the client's card through the reader as well as the legal POS-terminal.

Or you can hack into the processing center of a bank or a large retail chain that operates transactions by actual shops, hotels, and restaurants, and you steal the client database. Or you can simply buy the dumps from people that use one of these two ways."

"But you have to write the dumps onto the credit card itself…"

"Of course. To do that, you need another piece of equipment, called an encoder. They're sold legally and cost about $900. You simply connect it to your computer with a USB cord, punch the dump into a simple program, swipe the card — and voila, you're holding a magnetic copy of some American Richie Rich's card."

"And off you go to the shop?" concluded Galina.

"No, it's a little early for shopping at this point. Your card may be a working copy, but it's still just a piece of white plastic. A cashier will be really surprised if you try to pay with that."

"So, what do you do?"

"You make a deal with a cashier at some nice shop. Something along the lines of 'hey, I've got this thing here. What about I buy a laptop and a plasma TV, then we sell them and split the money?' It works — owners of restaurants, boutiques and casinos gave us up to 50% of the money we cashed, and we told them what to tell their bank if they have problems."

"What problems?"

"Sooner or later the real cardholder will complain. He'll contact his bank, they will contact Visa, and before you know it the bank that installed the POS-terminal sends security to your doorstep. 'You've been very naughty cashing all those fake cards,' they'll say. This is the part where our manager makes a surprised face and says, 'I don't know anything. Talk to the girl that was working the register yesterday.' He calls the girl over. The bank people will ask her,

'Have you checked the validity period?'

'Of course!'

'And the signature on the back of the card?'

'Sure. I even made sure it matched the one in his passport. And he put the same signature on the slip.'"

"What slip?" My lawyer had to be explained everything like a preschooler.

"The receipt, that you get after paying for something with a credit card, is called a *slip*. It holds all the information about the purchase: time, date, organization name, details of the place of the purchase. By the way, the information for the slip is taken from the track1. And while the dump doesn't care, what name you put on track1 — the actual cardholder's name or the name from your fake passport — the card number must be real, otherwise the transaction simply won't work. Would be pretty sweet otherwise, you just need to get a fake passport, take it to any bank in just about any country and get an account with a debit card. As a result you get a card of some John Smith with $5 on it and a passport for the same name with your photo in it. Then you erase all the data from the magnetic stripe, get a dump from the base, change the name in track1 to John Smith and off you go to a bank or a shop. Once this dump runs out of money, you erase it, prepare a new one and record it. That may continue until all those shops and banks all over the world start looking for that John Smith. Then you simply get a new passport and start over. After everyone learns your face, you can get a plastic surgery and go on."

Galina laughed out.

"When the people from the bank ask the cashier if she made sure the card number and the cardholder name on the receipt matched those on the card, she'll say 'sure'. She'll add that the card wasn't damaged and didn't look counterfeit. They won't have any more questions after that. The bank can suspect all they want, but they have no legal reasons to block the transaction.

Of course, if the cashiers actually checked that the information on the card matched that on the slip, it would be impossible to use the same card multiple times. But in the country of fearless idiots, also known as Belarus, the cashiers didn't bother to follow the rules, and I could often get away with cashing dumps recorded on genuine, but expired cards, and sometimes even on discount cards. We didn't 'milk' one place too often — the bank may have taken away the terminal and leave us out of job completely.

"What is 'white plastic'? Is it the same 'plastic' that they allegedly found at you place?"

"They got it from Saprykin. And he told the cops I gave it to him along with PIN-codes and asked to get some cash from Minsk ATMs. I hope, you know what a PIN-code is?"

"I do. The four digits that you need to get cash out of an ATM."

"Right."

"Where did you get the PINs?"

"The average cardholder is convinced that PIN-codes are impossible to hack or steal, but I could name about ten ways to do just that."

"Wow! What ways?" Galina wasn't hiding her interest.

"Can we talk it about next time? It's a huge topic, and I'm tired, I'd like to go back to the cell."

"I can pass a letter to your family."

"Right. Give me a minute to write something."

I write:

> *"Hello, Foxy! I'm alright, hanging in there. I'm more worried about you. I've received your letter and written a reply — you'll get it soon. Can you please number the letters you write, and I'll do the same, so we won't have to guess if everything has been delivered. I also got your care package, thanks a lot. Contact Kaizer, he owes me $10,000, tell him to give it to you. Find the guy from St. Petersburg — he owes me another ten.*
>
> *About Ilya Saprykin. Tell him to sell the office and return the money I invested, I'm not taking 'no' for an answer.*
>
> *Tell Dmitry to change passwords to all my ICQ accounts (I bet the cops are all over them) and tell the clients to beware of the cops. Do that ASAP. Tell everyone I said Hi. Love you lots."*

"Make sure you hide it well," I told the lawyer.

"Do you mind if I read it first?"

I nodded. Galina skimmed the note, folded it and put it in her bra.

"Who's going to search an old woman's underwear?" she reacted to my surprise.

I agreed.

"I'll be back tomorrow and we'll talk more, carder," she pronounced the last word slowly, as if trying to remember it.

CHAPTER 4

VOLODARKA, OH VOLODARKA

Minsk City Pre-trial Detention Center ("Volodarka")

Prisons are different from each other just like households are. They have different moods, food, the whole spectrum of feelings you have while being there varies from family to family. But as far as general distinction is concerned, there are only two types of prisons — the "red" ones and the "black" ones. At the red ones the administration holds all the power, which means the conditions are always strict. As for the black ones, they are practically under control of the authoritative convicts that, however, act with the acquiescence of the actual prison authorities. Volodarka of that period was, to my huge relief, a "black" prison.

The first thing that happens to you at the Pre-trial Detention Center is a body search. They break apart the arch supports in your shoes, which sometimes cost more than the average prison guard makes a month. You're also stripped of all forbidden items including belts and shoe laces. The only answer you get to your timid protests is "Against the rules. Don't want you to hang yourself on those in the cell." However, the cops know better than anyone else how sweaters, hats and even synthetic socks (those make the strongest thread) will give you enough material to make a rope. After all, if you're desperate enough to hang yourself, even a bed sheet will do.

"Undress. Underwear too. Stretch your arms forward. Squat three times (in case you're hiding something forbidden between your buttcheeks). Get dressed, move along. Next."

The next thing that awaits you is the Special Unit — a mug shot, fingerprints again, then personal details. Then you get to the holding cell. To be frank, it must be one of the most notable parts of the prison. It is a huge cell, but it hasn't got any plank beds (instead, it's got a 'stage' — a platform made of boards, sloppily put together), and everyone is placed there as soon as they arrive to the prison. In a few days (up to 6 if you were unlucky to arrive during a national holiday) people are moved to their cells according to their offences: low security (for first-timers) or high security (for repeat offenders). The most obvious reason for such division is not to let the experienced criminals 'educate' the new ones.

When Soviet writer Sergey Dovlatov was asked what the worst thing about a Soviet prison was, he answered: "To relieve myself in a roomful of people." Let me remind you that he served his time in mid-1970s. Four decades later, people have learnt to make computers as small as a watch, but the prison toilets of the former USSR remain the same — in the open. And while there are improvised solutions in the cells (such as a hand-made rope and a bed sheet), at the holding cell you'll just have to put up with it.

A description this detailed may put off people that are fond of action stories. They should probably just skip these pages. However, these first impressions as I was getting to know my new home I believe, must be told just as they really were.

Next day, they took us to the shower rooms (we were allowed to take a shower), took a blood sample (for HIV and syphilis tests), and a TB test. I guess I was really lucky: I only spent one day at the holding cell, and the following day we were pulled out in groups of five to six people and escorted somewhere else.

Prison corridors, filled with liquid electric light, looked surprisingly spacious. On both sides were dark rectangles of doors with huge bars and numbers of cells, and it was difficult to imagine that every door was hiding a cell housing up to 30 people.

First, we were taken to the warehouse where we were given everything we needed: a mattress as thick as a flat sheet, a pillow, a woolen duvet so worn out it had holes in it, an aluminum spoon with a broken off handle and a similarly handleless mug. I marched a little further down the corridor and a moment later a heavy metal door with a *feeder* (a small window to pass food, care packages and letters from home into the cell) closed behind my back with a dull thud.

"Hey, guys!" — I stood in the doorway somewhat at a loss.

"Hello," someone greeted me from inside the cell. "What are you here for?"

"212th."

"What's that?"

"Computer fraud…"

"What are you, a hacker or something?"

"Not exactly."

"Come on in then."

Only now I could finally see who I was talking to. I could have done it sooner if it wasn't for the thick cigarette smoke that filled up the cell. It was a lanky guy in his early twenties, covered in tattoos.

"Makar," he introduced himself. "I look after this cell. What's your name?"

"Sergey."

"Oh, a namesake. Where are you from?"

"Minsk."

Did they keep you long at the holding cell?"

"Nah, I was just brought in yesterday and today they tossed me in here. The rest were there since Friday."

"Do you know what cell this is?"

"No."

"Shame," Makar shook his head in disapproval. "The number of the cell is on the wall behind the cell door. They could have put you in with the cocks, what would you have done then?"

"Don't know. Kill myself, I guess."

"Cocks" is the term used by the prison community for forced passive homosexuals. In the holding cell, more experienced convicts said that sometimes cops would intentionally assign you to a "gay" cell to break your spirit. And if, God forbid, you do end up in that cell, you have to break out of there by all means necessary. Because you can be "brought down" and "turned", and the others will never let you undo or forget it. Being "turned" is the worst punishment of all. It often happens at the pre-trial detention centers when a police informant (or someone seriously suspected of being one) is brought there. It can also happen to a "rat" — someone who has stolen from his cellmates. It will inevitably happen to pedophiles and other sex offenders. It's a horrible revenge, since there's no way to go back. Cocks can't be taken from. You can give him something, but don't even think about accepting anything from him; otherwise you can be turned into one as well. They're much like India's untouchables. At prison camps, the cocks do the hardest and most humiliating jobs: they sweep and clean, take out the trash and clear snow, wash toilets and every corner of the barracks. They eat separately from everyone else, they have their own dishes, and they sleep separately as well — usually at the doorway in the barracks or under the beds or the clothes rack. Bored prisoners can punch or bully them. They're often used for sex (the "working cocks") — for tea or a few cigarettes or chocolates.

"Could you?" the shot caller watched me with interest.

"I could," I unclenched my fist and showed them a sharp narrow blade from a disposable razor that I had kept in my mouth.

"Alright. You can take that plank to rest," he pointed at a bed in the center of the cell. "You'll share it with one more guy. His name's Igor, you can take turns to rest, 12 hours each. It's not too bad,"

Makar must have noticed the surprised look on my face. "In other cells, some sleep in three shifts. Sort out the schedule between you two, we're a community based on mutual understanding here. The guys will tell you about our routines, ask me if you have any questions. Alright, bro, get some rest, we'll talk later."

The man I had to share my plank with was about forty and the details of all the parties he'd been to could be read in the scars on his closely cropped head.

I put down my bag, a massive checkered bag Soviet shuttle traders used to take to Poland, in the corner of the cell, sat at the edge of my plank, took a deep breath and looked around. The room was lit by a single dim yellow bulb in a thin metal net. There were four bunk plank beds, a flush toilet in the corner, a cold water tap right above it and a small barred window. The cell was small (not more than 15 square meters) and crowded — there were people on all the bunk beds. It smelt of unwashed bodies, dirty socks and cigarette smoke. There was no ventilation whatsoever, and every single inmate smoked.

The planks were so close to each other you could only squeeze between them if you moved sideways. Some of them were covered with thin blankets, some were open, but the clothes thrown over ropes for drying made it hard to estimate how many people were on the top bunks. I later found out there were 13 of us. I've read somewhere that prison sanitary standards allow at least two square meters for every prisoner — at Volodarka at that time the norm was reduced to less than one.

My world had narrowed to the size of the cell. Somewhere outside, big city life was humming: herds of cars were scurrying down the streets, contracts were being signed in banks and offices, exams were being taken, babies born. But none of it had anything to do with me. For the first time in my life I was entirely separated from the society.

CHAPTER 5

NO FENCE AGAINST A FAIL

Chifir is a very strong black tea. According to an old prison tradition, we all drank from the same mug, two sips each. The sips didn't come easy (try adding 40-50 g of loose black tea to 200 ml of water), but it gave you such energy, that 10 minutes later I could feel the hairs on my arms move.

"Are you expecting anyone today?" asked Igor, the guy that I shared the plank bed with.

"The lawyer promised to come, but I'm not sure when. Why?"

"I'll give you my wife's number. Ask your lawyer to tell her to send me a care package."

"No problem."

An hour later I was tossed out of the cell. Galina brought a scent of some expensive, but old-fashioned French perfume with herself. It smelt very familiar.

"Hello, Sergey," she greeted me. "How did your first night in prison go?"

"It wasn't my first one — I had spent a night in the holding cell. But this one's the first in my new cell, yes. It was alright, at least I got some sleep. Slept for fourteen hours straight."

"I've passed your note to Katya, she wrote you a few lines back. She's alright. Dmitry too."

"Have Kaizer and Fidel left?"

"Yes, they were all let go the same day."

"Thank God," I breathed a sigh of relief: my friends were free.

"Your mother is very worried about you. She's asking why you don't write to her."

"I can't think of what to write to her. I guess I'm ashamed. I got into prison, after all. A criminal case as well."

"You'd better stop that," Galina reassured me. "No fence against a fail, remember? Even millionaires do their time."

"Alright. Tell her I'll write."

"Good man. Where did we leave off?"

"We were educating you about bank cards."

"Right. You told me how they worked, about dumps and how you could cash out white plastic through associates at shops, casinos, etc. How else do you steal money from credit cards?"

"Here's a real power players' strategy: you make a suitcase full of white plastic with recorded dumps, open a fake company, rent an office, buy some electronic goods and go into business. The prices at your store are low, word-of-mouth advertising works perfectly, and the client flock in. You open a bank account, sign a contract and install a POS-terminal. We start swiping our customers' cards, and our own credit cards from different banks — we make sure the bank gets used to large amounts of credit card purchases. Then one day we run the said suitcase of white plastic through the terminal, the money gets into the account, we cash it and get the hell out of there.

Of course, it's not all that easy, first you have to study the country where you want to do this. Find out about the possible pitfalls: the security systems of the bank that installed your POS-terminal, how long it takes for your hard-earned money to get into your account (the faster the better), think of escape routes, count the expenses — and a lot more. It goes without saying that you can't register the company under your real name."

"But it all has little to do with what's in your charges. You are accused of purchasing goods at stores of Minsk, using counterfeit cards…"

"Okay, let's move on to more complex things. How can we make a credit card that looks legitimate enough to take it to any store in any country?

First, you buy ready-made plastic with 'doves' or a 'globe'. You can also buy those holograms separately. Then you either find a typography or buy your own equipment that will help you print something pretty on the CR-80 plastic. As a rule, it doesn't matter one bit, what bank's name is on the card, and if it matches the real one. The printing, of course, has to be double-sided. Finally, we got it printed. Now we need to make those dented card number, cardholder's name and such — we'll have to buy an embosser (a machine that dents digits into plastic cards) and a tipper (a machine that makes them look gold or silver). Expensive embossers will have a built-in tipper. In addition to all that, you'll have to put a piece of special paper for the owner's signature on the back of the card."

"That sounds like a lot of money…" Galina noted, absent-mindedly.

"That's right. A good embosser, Matika Z3, for example, if going to cost you about ten grand. So I've never made the plastic myself, always bought it from specialists. Boa Factory in Kyiv sells low-quality cards that are good enough to shop in former Soviet countries, Flint from RealPlastic.org makes great Visa Electron, and the Chinese make the best offset plastic. But kudos to the Internet for allowing us to work with pretty much anyone, anywhere in the world. Of course, I had to record dumps onto the plastic myself — we don't trust this kind of intimate matter to the plastic manufacturers.

So, before you know it, you've got a suitcase full of credit card duplicates that look genuine. What do you do with that suitcase? You buy a ticket to Singapore or Pretoria and go on a massive shopping spree until the suitcase is empty. Or even better — to Italy, the Mecca of counterfeit credit cards. In Milan, if the shop assistant finds out the card is fake, he won't call the police. In fact, he'll encourage you to use it to buy as much as possible, because he knows the bank will make amends. Then you get rid of the goods: you sell some, you give some away. Then you change country. Then you do it all again with a new passport and new credit cards. We went shopping in Minsk, Belarus. We shouldn't have, of course — never steal where you live.

You should also check the dumps from time to time between visits to stores. Because what you don't want is the POS-terminal to show the code 43 (stolen card — pick up and contact the authorization center) or 07 (pick up the card and try to hold the fraudulent cardholder)."

"Alright, Sergey," my lawyer said, "we've sorted out the shopping cards. Now what about the PINs? Saprykin claims it was you who gave him 20 white cards, wrote PINs in permanent marker on each and asked him to use them to take out cash them at Minsk ATMs. Is that true?"

"Yes and no."

"What do you mean?"

"Saprykin's got a finger in the pie himself."

"Alright, the investigation will tell. But at the moment he's a witness — against you."

"I've heard witnesses very often become defendants."

"You're not going to sink him, are you? What you definitely don't need is a conspiracy charge. So, where did you get the PIN-codes?"

CHAPTER 6

ROADS

One of the cells at Volodarka prison where I spent over 3 weeks

There was no TV in the cell. There were no board games either, except the chess set we made from bread. Our cell, No. 144, was mostly made up of drug addicts. The overseer of the cell, Sergey Makarov, was an injection drug user with a long history of addiction despite being only 25 years old. He'd shoot anything illegal up his vein. If Aspirin was illegal, he'd get high on it too. He told me that while Belarusian druggies used to use heroin and methadone, today's most popular high was from the opium poppy seeds that normal people use to decorate their cakes.

"We got that from Russia," Makar told me one evening over a cup of chifir. "By law, all poppy seeds for food production must undergo heat treatment to destroy opium. However, in reality, they only do it to about 10% of all the poppy seeds."

"Have you got any accomplices?" Makar jumped to another topic.

"Yes," I sighed, "unfortunately. One is under a pledge not to leave the country, the other is somewhere here."

"Accomplices are bad," Makar said thoughtfully. "There's nothing worse than when somebody is trying to get his hands clean and doesn't mind sinking everyone else in the process. Cops love it. Nah, if you break the law — do it yourself. Being alone is safer in a lot of ways. Which cell is he in?"

"Who?"

"Your associate."

"I don't know yet. I'll ask him if I see him somewhere."

"You can write a search note," Makar explained. "It will go through all the cells, and we might find your boy."

I wrote one of these search notes, carefully coated it with a few layers of cigarette packet wrapper and melted the edges with a lighter — the *road* in our cell was a wet one — through the toilet bowl. How exactly do *roads* — the prison post — work? First you need a *horse* — a self-made rope from unpicked knitted clothes. You do it by twisting — you put four or five thin threads together and twist them, then fold them in two and twist again — that gives you a thin and relatively strong rope. You attach *hedgehogs* (spiky balls made of matches) or *floaters* (toilet paper packed into cigarette pack wrap) to its end. Guys in the cell next door do the same. Then both horses go down the toilet, where they get into the sewer after you flush them down with massive amounts of water. There they interlock. The *road* is ready. Later one of the *horses* is removed, and the other is used to transfer notes and packages — mostly tea and cigarettes.

It takes a search note an average of two days to go through all cells. I've sent it twice, and no cell turned out to contain my associate or even anybody who knew a Pavel Voropayev.

CHAPTER 7

DARK ELVIS

"Let's return to PIN-codes," suggested my lawyer during her next visit. "Where did you get PIN-codes for the cards?"

In his time Boa — the best carder in the world — said, "don't believe your eyes the next time you see someone selling dumps with PINs. Dumps with PINs are basically cash. And I don't see people selling $100 for $20." The first person to prove him wrong was Dark Elvis.

It all started one morning when my ICQ began exploding with heaps of messages from colleagues, partners and customers. They all wanted to know the same thing:

"Do you know Dark Elvis?"

"Bro, are you Dark Elvis?"

"Help me find Dark Elvis pls."

"Who the hell is Dark Elevis?" I boiled over. "Why is everybody suddenly so interested in him?"

"Everyone being…" eNdi, my Spanish partner, was curious.

"Andycredit asked in the morning, then Mondeo, now you…"

"Bro, are you well? You're usually the first to find out about everything. Elvis sells dumps with PINs."

"That's too good to be true."

Dark Elvis was like a UFO — a mysterious object everyone knew about, but nobody could find. We didn't even know anything about him except his nickname. However, somehow everyone did know that Elvis had tens of thousands of dumps with PINs.

"Auger, could you tell me Dark Elvis's contacts?" I wrote to one of my regular dumps supplier.

"Are you kidding?" he reacted almost momentarily.

"Does it look like I'm kidding?"

"Never mind. I won't give you his contacts, but you can work with him through me. What are you interested in?"

"Same thing everyone is interested in — dumps with PINs."

"I can email you a couple. You can try them out and pay me $600 if they're alright. Deal?"

"Deal."

In a few hours Auger sent me two American debit dumps with PIN-codes. A Maestro and a Visa Classic.

"When will you check them?"

"Now. I've got an encoder."

Forty minutes later I was already gutting one of Kyiv's ATMs. The Visa didn't work, but the Maestro gave me $3000. The ATM seemed reluctant to give me the remaining $600 — the balance check showed there was a total of $3600 on the card. I guessed the daily limit must have been $3000.

"So how did it go?" my ICQ window flashed a message from Auger as soon as I got home and turned on my computer.

"Alright. Classic didn't work, but Maestro was okay."

"That's $300 then. You know my wallet number."

"There you go," I opened my WebMoney wallet and sent $300 to Auger.

"Got it. Thanks. Do you still want to get in touch with Dark Elvis?"

"I don't really care who to work with. I can work with you, if you don't want to hand over his contacts."

"Let's work together," Auger agreed. "Here are the conditions."

That's where he disappointed me a little: one European dump with a PIN cost $2000, no refunds on faulty ones (unlike the trial purchase), a minimum order was 10 dumps. Take it or leave it.

I tried it once, spent $20,000. It wasn't too bad, but I made no profit because of the faulty dumps. I'm not playing that lottery again.

"I still believe that Auger was the mythical Dark Elvis…"

"What Auger?" Galina didn't have the access to my memory.

"Auger, my dump supplier. The one who sold me dumps with PIN-codes."

"OK. And why are you sure that Dark Elvis and Auger are the same person?"

"Most likely Auger — a top-class cybercriminal with years of experience — had a few nicknames that even his partners in illegal business didn't connect to each other and believed to be different people."

CHAPTER 8

EVERYBODY LIES

"How can you decrypt PINs?" — Galina interrupted my musings.

"The first and uppermost rule payment systems have for storing and transferring PIN-codes is that their digits must be encrypted at all times. From the moment they're punched in at the ATM or a POS-terminal to the moment they're checked by the payment system. Access is strictly restricted, both physically (there are break-in-resistant modules) and digitally."

"So, how do you do it?"

"At different stages of processing, PIN-codes go through different steps of encryption and decryption. If you can find flaws in the interface you can hack into it at one of the intermediate servers. The rest is easy — you install a *sniffer* — a program that intercepts PIN-codes either decrypted, or encrypted, but available for decrypting. Carrying out a hack like that may take up to a few years."

"Why don't they patch up those flaws?" my lawyer asked the most reasonable question.

"The people who install and set up the systems aren't always honest or qualified enough, and that is what makes the systems vulnerable. Sometimes you don't even have to hack anything — due to developers' neglect programs that are used by shops for bank card processing sometimes save not only the dumps, but also the PIN-codes."

"So, the bankers aren't completely honest when they say PIN-codes are unhackable…"

"Everyone lies."

"What about the PINs they found at Saprykin's," Galina moved on to pragmatic matters, "where did they come from?"

"In early 2004 I met Black Monarch — one of moderators at Carder.org, the world's first forum for carders. He was selling American dumps with PIN-codes, but only among people he knew since he couldn't get too many — only about 500 a month."

"Good grief! How did you cash all that?"

"We gave them to cash mules in different countries, let them keep 15-30%, and they sent our share via Western Union. All of them, except the people that lived nearby and could be controlled personally, screwed us over and kept huge amount for themselves. It is practically impossible to check how much money was cashed off your dump."

"You said Black Monarch was selling dumps with PINs. How did he get them?" my lawyer perked up.

"In short, we take a dump with an original Track1, which has the cardholder's real name. We can use this to find his social security number, date of birth, home address and phone number — the more information we get the better. It goes without saying that if the cardholder's name is John Smith, we'll never figure out which of the two thousand Accurint search results is our guy, so you should go for a last name that's unusual. Then we go to the website of the bank that issued the card and change its PIN. However, you can't change the PIN on all cards. Those cards, with known balance we sold for 15% of their balance.

When I had absolutely nothing to do, I'd call the victims on Skype and try to get their PIN-codes. You can also do it automatically: a cardholder receives a phone call where a program reads a text in a robotic voice, warns them about suspicious activity with their bank account and instructs them to say the credit card number, its expiry date and PIN-code."

"Where do you get the social security number and other personal data?"

"There are plenty of people on carding forums that have turned disclosing Americans' personal data into a profession. It will cost you $3-5 per person. Why Americans? Because databases with full information on citizens, including marriages and divorces, criminal records, place of employment, movable and immovable assets, registered weapons, credit history, and so on only exist in the States. There is no unified database for the European Union, only separate countries. Also, there are about 300 million potential victims in the States, while there are only 10 million in, say, Belgium. The odds are much better."

"How else can you find out a PIN-code?"

"Phishing has been getting increasingly popular recently."

"What's phishing?"

"The word comes from the word 'fishing'. Users get emails that include duplicate web pages of their banks, payment systems, social networking sites and so on, where the plotter can get valuable personal info (logins and passwords, credit card numbers, PIN-codes, access to various paid websites). Technically, phishing is a classic con-art, the art of pretending to be someone you're not. It is based on the fact that the users don't know very basic things — e.g. banks and payment services never send out emails asking you to give them any details. Phishing is particularly popular in the USA, where people are law-abiding: if a bank has sent a form, you must fill it out."

"And what do the PINs have to do with phishing?" my lawyer was still clueless.

"A lot of phishers have massive stores of cards with corresponding PIN-codes. Card numbers, not dumps, mind you. And we, carders, had the dumps — some of us had as many as a few million. My idea was to find matches between databases of cards and dumps. We matched them by the card number."

"Did it work?"

"You bet. Only as much as 0.3% matched, but given that phishers and carders had millions of cards and dumps between them, that gave me a pretty sweet income."

"Are those all the ways to get PIN-codes?"

"No. Another way to get a PIN-code is called trapping. You go to an ATM, put in your card, punch in the PIN-code and…nothing happens. You keep standing there wondering what went wrong. Inevitably a stranger will come up and ask if there's anything wrong with the ATM. You try to explain and punch in your PIN-code again, right in front of him. You can't cash out any money or get your card out — it's simply stuck. You get angry and go to the bank's office to find out what the hell is wrong with the machine.

When you leave, the stranger pulls out a thin strip of photo film that was inside it and didn't let the ATM read your card along with the card. And he already knows the PIN-code! And then there's skimming.

"And what's what?"

"Skimming is one of the types of carding most hated by bankers. A skimmer is a tiny device only a few millimeters thick that you put into the card slot of an ATM. It looks just like the card reader, so an average person won't know the difference. The victim inserts the card into the ATM and doesn't suspect he's actually dealing with a well-concealed skimmer that reads the card's dump and saves it."

"Wait, what about the PIN-code? The skimmer only copies the dump, right?"

"Figuring out the PIN in this case is an art form of itself. Criminals use concealed video cameras or even keyboard replicas that go over real ones. Some rules: don't install a skimmer in the morning: people tend to be more vigilant at that time. Don't choose an ATM that serves over 250 people a day. Avoid cities with less than 15,000 people — the locals know what their ATMs look like and may notice your skimmer.

By the way, do you know which cell Pavel Voropayev is in?" I changed the topic.

"I don't, and I'd be careful if I were you," Galina warned me. "He's got the same lawyer as his associate, your friend Batyuk, and that's only possible if they've got the same strategy. And that strategy is most likely sinking you. They can even claim you organized the whole thing and if they both tell the same story; the judge is going to believe them."

CHAPTER 9

TOO BIG FOR MINSK

How did I get myself into this mess? Had I not got myself involved with Pavel Voropayev and Stepan Batyuk I wouldn't have been noticed, and I definitely wouldn't have been under investigation. They were both short of fake credit cards and they didn't have any money to order any new ones. All they had were a couple of new laptops and strong desire to work as my cash mules.

So, I contacted Igor Liratto, one of the owners of BoaFactory.net — a Kyiv outlet specializing in counterfeit credit cards and various documents, from college diplomas to passports. Boa Factory's website was generously decorated with tempting offers like "Want a Russian passport in three days? No problem!", "Need a college diploma? Easy!", "Certificates, visas, all kinds of licenses? You came to the right place, buddy!" Boa Factory offered counterfeit documents of any kind, made so well they were impossible to tell apart from authentic ones. The prices varied greatly depending on the quality. A Russian passport, for example, was about $400, while Irish citizenship (despite the fact you got it the wrong way) would cost you $25,000. Boa Factory worked with "real plastic", selling both ready-made credit cards and equipment you need to make your own.

"Igor, have you got any encoders in store?" I asked.

"Yeh, no problem."

"I don't have the money though…"

"What do you mean?"

"What I've just said. I've got a laptop, Toshiba Satellite, new, still in the box. Take it as a deposit. Once we're done with the plastic, I'll exchange it for money."

"Alright, come over."

A few days later Stepan and I were in Kyiv. I must admit, the capital of Ukraine has left a lasting impression. After quiet Minsk that seems stuck in the Soviet Union, Kyiv looked like Europe. Countless affordable cafes, huge malls, sky scrapers, exhibitions, humming nightlife — you could feel the freedom everywhere, from the air to the minds of the people.

We spent a few days drinking the strongest Austrian rum in the company of young, but talented carders from Carder.org — Neo, Motherfucker and Leeloo (who turned out to be a very sweet girl called Olga) and sharing experiences. After the three-day drinking spree, I finally met Igor, exchanged the laptop for the encoder and returned to Minsk with a feeling of satisfaction at a job well done.

From then on, we were very busy. We recorded a dump on a used bank card, cashed it quickly, erased the dump, recoded a new dump over it and then repeated the whole thing. At that time American dumps, which cost $5-10, worked perfectly in Belarus. Thirty cases of vodka, a case of cognac, gold, a couple of cameras, Swiss watches, expensive delicious food, cigars, perfume, cell phones, petrol, restaurants and saunas — we paid for everything with fake credit cards. We got into it so much that we started to neglect basic precautions — cases of vodka were loaded right into our banker friend's cash microbus and we milked the same place for too long. The city grew too small for us — there were no places left where they'd accept credit cards and didn't know our faces. To be fair, there were only about 30 places that accepted credit cards in Minsk back in 2002.

CHAPTER 10

A LITTLE HOLIDAY

"Why don't we go on a shopping trip? Over here every dog knows our names," I suggested one morning after another haul that ended with an obligatory party with call-girls at a sauna. I know just the place: a Russian city where I spent a couple of very productive weeks last summer.

The following weekend we were loading our belongings onto a train: a laptop, an encoder, about a dozen cards from Boa Factory, some personal things and a few huge bags with vodka and food that we, again, paid for with our plastic.

Oleg, my old Internet friend, who we were going to stay with, met us at the train station and put us up in his one-bedroom apartment.

The money we had with us lasted a couple of days.

"Oleg, have you got a car?" I asked our host.

"No, why?"

"The place I'd like to work at is 120 kilometers away."

"My buddy has got one. Just pay for the petrol."

"Ask him to drive us on credit, we're all out of money," Stepan finally started to get into working mode. "We'll pay him once we make the money."

I called an old friend of mine that I worked with at the same location the previous summer:

"Anatoly, hi, it's me. Get yourself into shape, I've got a job for you. Tomorrow I'll be in your town. You got any decent clothes? A suit or something."

"I haven't got a suit, but I'll find something."

"Put on expensive shoes — people always pay attention to shoes. I'll give you my watch. You know what they say, first impression's half the battle. Get a haircut, shave and make yourself look respectable like last time. I want you to look like an out-of-town millionaire. I'll see you tomorrow at ten, bro."

The following day the three of us were looking our best. Stepan was wearing a smart three-piece suit, while Pavel went for a "golden youth" look in an Adidas Original jacket, ragged jeans and a cap. We were waiting for Anatoly, who was late.

"Are you sure he'll manage?" Stepan was worried. "He's not punctual — that's a bad sign."

"Don't fuss," I wasn't going to let worry get the better of my guys. "They haven't got roads as we know them here, they're basically serpentines in the mountains. That's why he's late. He's an experienced mule — he worked perfectly last time. Pretends to be a rich guy from Moscow that spent a week drinking in the middle of nowhere and is trying to make it up with his wife. By buying jewelry in bulk. I was pretending to be his son. Worked like a charm."

Anatoly showed up only half an hour later. He didn't look fresh at all.

"Sergey, bro!" he went in for a bear hug, "I've been waiting for you since you left. Let's do some work."

"Work your ass!" Stepan wasn't a fan of my old friend. "Have you seen yourself? You were asked to look decent! Much of a hangover? Fucker…"

"Stepan is right! You need a wash, new clothes, a make-over… Alright, Stepan, let the man be," I stepped in between them. "We'll get him up and running in to time. Come to think of it, this hangover and your five o'clock shadow will come in handy. Come here."

I took him to our car, thrust a shoe brush and a tube of polish into his hands, gave him a fresh shirt, a golden bracelet and took off my expensive watch and put it onto his wrist. As a final gesture, I sprayed some of my favorite Hugo Boss onto Anatoly's unshaved neck.

"All done," I gave my buddy a reassuring pat on the shoulder. "Have you picked shopping spots?"

"Sergey… the thing is…" Anatoly muttered. "Since we last worked together most shops removed their terminals and only accept cash now. There are only three or four places left where they accept plastic."

"Why didn't you tell me?!" I was so disappointed I thought I was going to cry.

"You never told me you were coming…"

That was true — we had travelled three thousand kilometers and I never bothered to call any locals to check out the situation. And at the moment I only had wind in my pockets: we needed to make some money just to return home.

"Alright. Anatoly, what places still accept plastic?"

"A cell phone shop, a couple of sports stores, a perfume store," my friend blurted out.

"Doesn't sound like much…"

We returned to Stepan and Pavel, who were smoking nervously.

"Guys, the thing is…" I started, losing confidence as I spoke. "There are almost no places to work at. So you, Stepan, are going to a mobile phone store. Pavel, you're going to the sports store, and I'll go with Anatoly, to cover him if something goes wrong. All clear?"

The guys nodded in agreement. I distributed the cards: Stepan got the best ones. We agreed to meet by the car or call each other if anything happened.

"So, I enter the store," Stepan was telling me hastily an hour later. "I look at stuff, I try out different phones, I talk to the shopping assistant. I've chosen five phones and ask for a discount. The manager agrees. I hand over the card — the cashier spends ages inspecting it, tries to lift the signature stripe with her fingernail, puts the card under a UV lamp, all that. She even checked my documents — I had a fake Estonian driving license and the cards in the same name. I nearly shat myself when she put that card under the UV lamp."

"The plastic went through all the checks perfectly. Then the cashier chilled a bit and put the card into the POS terminal. Then we were waiting for the result. Not just us — security by the door was waiting as well. Code 05 — decline. I give her another card — it gives code 01, call to bank. The girl picks up the phone and starts calling the bank. I think, to hell with this, I won't get so lucky second time around. I take the card back and ask her to put the phones into a bag while I get cash from my car. Then I just legged it. Idiots!"

"Alright, Pavel, what have you got?" I asked my other associate.

He said though there were POS terminals in the two sports stores that he visited, but they didn't work.

Anatoly said the same.

"Why didn't both cards work?" Stepan was addressing me, or himself — I couldn't tell. "It never happened in Minsk. Did you check the validity?" now he was clearly addressing me.

"A minute before you entered the shop."

"And where are their dumps from?"

"The States."

"So why don't we try European ones?" Stepan was displaying the quick wits one can't often expect of him. "What if the Yankee cards just don't work here?"

"Yeh, why don't we try European ones…" I replied, somewhat annoyed. "The American dumps worked last year."

Last year… I couldn't believe I actually said that! What an idiot! In the world of fake plastic everything can change overnight, and in our case it's been almost a year. Of course, I had "non-American" dumps on my PC back home — they were quite pricey, $50 — 100, but I think I had about five. The risk, however, was huge — given the vigilance the cashier at the cell phone shop had just shown, there's no doubt they're going to make sure the numbers on the card and the receipt match. We didn't have any new cards, so if we did get new dumps, we'd have to record them on the old cards. That's a dead giveaway.

"Anatoly, why don't we go to the same store that we bought clothes from last time? It's a designer shop with really expensive stuff — I bet they'll have a POS-terminal?" I asked, more to hear him confirm the decision I've already made in my mind.

"Alright, if you insist…"

"Let's meet here in an hour," I told the Minsk guys, and we parted ways.

I was feeling uneasy. It's definitely a bad idea to work at a place you've milked for $3,000 once… But we didn't have a choice.

Anatoly headed towards the shop. I was waiting for him to get about three hundred meters ahead and started to follow. We strolled down one street, then the next until we were standing in front of the store we needed. My buddy went in, and I kept watch on him from across the street. I didn't stand in one place, but kept walking up and down the street. Five minutes passed, then ten, then twenty, then half an hour, but my mule was nowhere to be seen. Instead, quite a number of shoppers in casual clothes appeared on the doorstep of the shop out of nowhere. It was a clear sign to head back. I went back to the car.

"Guy, we've got to hit the road!"

"Why?!" they were both staring at me.

"Before it's too late. Anatoly just got arrested."

We got into the car and returned to Oleg's place. I called Minsk as soon as possible, and we were sent $300 via Western Union. The train was leaving the same day. Unfortunately, $300 only got us two tickets, so Stepan and Pavel left, and I had to stay.

Anatoly knew Oleg's home phone number, so we all knew it was only a question of time before the cops showed up. We had to change apartments, quick. Oleg asked his girlfriend to host me for a few days, and stayed at home to wait for the cops. Before leaving I asked Oleg to take my bracelet and the watch from our failed mule. The visit from the cops went smoothly — they realized they had arrived too late and didn't turn the flat upside down. I waited for Monday, collected another money transfer at the Western Union office, took a taxi and went to the closest airport, which was 300 km away. I missed my flight by just a few minutes. So, I had to stay the night in the flimsy air terminal and wait for the morning flight. However, luck was still on my side, and I reached Moscow safely. Now, many years later, I can see another mistake we made: we bought our tickets with our real Belarusian passports. Had the police been a little more interested in catching us, they wouldn't have much trouble taking Pavel and Stepan off the train and meeting me at the airport.

CHAPTER 11

TWO AND A HALF YEARS?

"Now tell me more about the circumstances of your arrest. We'll try an appeal," Galina said at our next meeting.

"Have you asked the investigator if he is going to drop by?" I had my own questions.

"He will, don't worry. According to the law, a preliminary investigation lasts two months. For a grave crime like yours it may take up to 18 months. But I will call him and ask. How long have you been in the pre-trial detention already?"

"Almost two weeks."

"I see. I think he'll be here next week. I'll call you."

"What's his last name, by the way?"

"Makarevich. But now let's talk about your arrest."

"Up to eighteen months! And that's just the investigation." The idea of spending that much time here was frightening and wouldn't let me focus.

"And another year for the trial." My lawyer wasn't good at cheering people up. "At the most."

"Two and a half years in total. That's not fun at all."

"Well, I think it'll happen faster than that. At least I'm doing all I can to make sure it will."

"That's reassuring. When I was arrested, they gave me the duty lawyer. She just told straight up: 'I know your investigator, he's a good man, just tell him everything you've done.' Not great legal assistance."

"A frank confession softens the sentence, but increases jail time," Galina said.

"Have you always been a lawyer?"

"No. I worked in prosecution for 20 years."

"How much do you charge?"

"A visit here is $100. A day in court is double that."

"I see. What do you want to know about how I was arrested?

"Let's start from the beginning. When you were arrested, what were you told, where were you taken, what were you doing? And where were you a few hours before the arrest? Which friends of yours were present during the arrest? Every detail is important."

CHAPTER 12

ARREST

11th September 2004, half an hour before my arrest, Fidel

September 11th, 2004, was a big day for my brother and me. It was the day DumpsMarket, my carding forum, was created, and we wanted to celebrate it with our partners and close friends. Error32 and Fidel — owners of CarderPortal.org, another carding forum — arrived from Odessa, Kaizer, my DumpsMarket moderator, came from Yekaterinburg, Alexander Suvorov (JonnyHell), one of the world's best hackers, came from Estonia, Ilya Saprykin and others came from Minsk. I rented out a small private hotel with everything necessary: Russian and Turkish saunas, a swimming pool, six cosy rooms with massive beds and animal pelts on the floor, a parking lot, Wi-Fi, a billiard table, a space for paint ball, a nice sitting room with a fireplace, a fleet of cooks and a lake with huge carps and sturgeons we could fish out and cook on the grill. It was the done thing that whenever we met colleagues, the host paid for everything. Needless to say, the guests didn't come empty-handed. Kaizer gave us two bottles of Martell L'Or, exclusive cognac in Baccarat crystal bottles. The Odessans brought along a blow-up sex doll and proudly presented it to my brother.

Why did we have to bring the laptops? Because we assumed the clients wouldn't let us be — they needed dumps pretty much 24/7. At least Katya had the brains to hide the money, $25,000 — the cops would have taken it as a nice present. I was going to take it to my grandad's house — I had a metal case there in which I used to keep my savings in his backyard. Nobody knew, not even my family. There was a little less than $200,000 already. How will grandad take my arrest? No, I can't tell him what's happened, but I must let mum know. Fidel denied he even had a laptop with him in the first place, claiming he only brought his passport, phone and the return ticket. It was a good call — who knows what the cops might have found there. I guess I will have to take responsibility for everything. Fine, one extra laptop won't kill me. The thing is that everything on those laptops was supposed to be encrypted by BestCrypt, an encoding program all forums claimed was unhackable. I guess we'll see about that.

"Katya told me you were arrested at her country house," Galina yanked me out of my reminiscences. "Did you ask yourself, why there? Everyone else was allowed to leave. If it was only about you, they could have just arrested you at own home; simple and quiet. While they got the KGB involved."

In Belarus, the KGB (the Committee for State Security) are the security services, which have retained their Soviet-era name, with all its associations of surveillance and political repression. All other former Soviet countries have re-named their security services, even Russia where the domestic security services are the Federal Security Bureau, or FSB.

Wait, what does the KGB have to do with all of this?! As far as I know, carders are the responsibility of the police. However, there was a KGB man during the arrest, I remember checking his documents. About 30 years old, short haircut, black leather jacket — I'd have assumed he was mafia if I had I seen him in the street.

"As far as I know, they were after you ever since your big party," my lawyer tossed at me another piece of puzzle.

Weird. Definitely weird.

"Alright, Sergey, don't rack your brains over it," Galina must have noticed the perplexed look on my face. "They've shown me an investigative report from the Minsk KGB. It went something along the lines of:

> 16th September 2004 we received information that a group of young men, including Pavlovich, suspected of committing a grave crime, left Minsk at about 6 p.m. in a Mercedes, number plate 9999TE, and headed in the direction of the Ukrainian border. We urge you to do everything possible to arrest Pavlovich on the Minsk-Gomel highway.

The KGB sent that report to the local police, knowing you would have to pass through the town on your way to Ukraine. They were supposed to arrest you in Osipovichi, but, apparently, that didn't work out."

"Well, the traffic police did stop me, but they let me go. When were they sent that order? After 6 p.m. I guess they sent it by fax, which means it was received immediately. It takes me about 40 minutes to reach Osipovichi. Looks like the traffic police weren't told in time."

"Looks like it," my lawyer agreed.

When they handcuffed me, I was still trying to laugh it off. I had dinner in handcuffs, had a shot of vodka — who knows when another chance will present itself — then I was put in the back of my own car and driven to the Osipovichi District Police Department, about 10 minutes away. There they put us in different rooms and searched our pockets. I happened to have $800 on me — officers spread the banknotes out on the table and kept photographing them. One investigator tried to take a picture of me, but I covered my face. Then they yanked us out into the front yard one by one — I remember the dreadful weather with strong wind and rain in my face — to inspect our cars. They ever brought some witnesses — some drunks from the temporary holding cell. There was nothing in my car. Nothing in Katya's either. Saprykin's BMW was searched last. Who would have thought he would have a cigarette pack full of white plastic we used two weeks ago? With PIN-codes written over the cards in permanent marker. And he knew it was in his car. Why didn't he just throw it out the window on his way to the Department, asshole? That was it. Into the different rooms again: what, how much, how, whose? Of course, I didn't say anything. Everyone was fingerprinted, then we were taken to some kind of an assembly hall.

From there we were taken to Minsk, the capital of our country. I dozed off in the back seat of my Mercedes. They hadn't taken off my handcuffs. As I later found out, Saprykin and his girlfriend were allowed to go back to Osipovichi. The rest were taken to Minsk City Police Department, seated on chairs (it was already 8 a.m.) and we spent the next three hours sitting in front of a police officer who was making sure we didn't talk to each other. Of course, we chatted anyway — the cop wasn't very particular about his duties. I was whispering sweet nothings into Katya's ear and giving last directions. Fidel was doing his best to cheer everyone up. Dmitry sat in silence. Kaizer was more worried than anyone else. Everyone was very tired — none of us got any sleep that night.

When it was almost 10 a.m. an investigator called Makarevich came about. Different rooms again. Fidel was questioned in a room next door and I could hear him shouting at the cops, "Sergey is a good chap, let him go". And when the cops were taking him away, he told me, 'Don't worry, we'll get you out of here'. Dmitry was trying to keep cool too, he waved at me as if trying to say that everything's going to be alright. Of course it is. The question is, when.

Then I was transferred to the temporary detention facility and spent the weekend there. What a shithole. The radio was turned on at 6 a.m. to broadcast the national anthem. Of course, I don't mind our anthem, it wouldn't be half as bad if it wasn't so loud. It was also the middle of the harvesting season and by the end of the first day I could already tell you exactly how much grain was harvested in each region.

On Sunday, they put a snitch in my room, but I didn't talk to him about my case. It wasn't like he was trying to pressure me into talking, he was more the quiet, listening type. Some of them were probably wired up.

"How do you know?" asked the lawyer.

"A few people I know have been to jail…"

After lunch, we went to the prosecutor's office. I entered the office still wearing handcuffs.

'Do you admit your guilt?' a man fat beyond his years asked me, unwillingly taking his eyes off his papers.

'No.'

'So you're going to go to jail?' he looked at me, surprised.

'Are there other options?'

There were no other options, so I ended up here," I finished my story and looked at the lawyer who was giving me the same look a snake typically gives its prey.

"That gives little hope," she nodded her head. "But we'll write something anyway — paper can't refuse ink."

"How are we going to mount a defense?"

"Deny everything. We'll get familiar with the text of prosecution, see what facts the investigation has, and only after that will you testify. Our judges hate it when your testimonies don't match: when you say one thing during the arrest, another thing at the preliminary hearing, and a third in court. Everyone sees you're lying and trying to wiggle your way out. A court hearing is a little show, and the more sympathy people have for your honesty, the better. That's why you should say the truth and only the truth in court. Just maybe not the whole truth."

"Alright, love, I need to go," my lawyer suddenly started to hurry away. "I will try to ask my people about the investigation. Katya said she had arranged your transfer to another cell — she seemed very concerned by the conditions you described. Do you want that transfer?"

"Yes," I answered.

"See you later, then. Hang in there."

The next day I was transferred to another cell.

CHAPTER 13

BADB

BadB has always loved making big gestures. Here he's on his yacht in Monaco.

In Moscow I met one of the founding fathers of CarderPlanet forum, known as BadB. We had been working together for quite some time at that point, but only online — either I bought his dumps or he bought mine.

There are a lot of people, particularly in the West, who think that Russian hackers and cyber-criminals in general, are nerds who sit in front of computers for hours a day and hack into something. More often than not, it isn't like this. Russian cyber-criminals look and behave like bandits, they're like wannabe gangsters: they socialize with criminal authorities and listen to prison songs.

The best Russian hackers that I knew were from the cities of Siberia and the north: Chelyabinsk, Zlatoust, Novosibirsk and Syktyvkar (Scorpo and Nicron where from around here). Many were very technically-minded, had taken maths or physics at universities and colleges and had engineer parents. Personally, I think there's a link between the prowess of their hackers and the short days and cold climate in this part of the world — which means kids spend a lot of time with computers. But hackers in Russia also thrive because the police do not have enough resources to find murderers, let alone hunt hackers. If a Russian hacker is found by the police, it's more likely to be the FBI or a European law enforcement agency — but Russia never extradites such suspects. If the Russian police do find them, then there's no need to go to prison: usually it's easy enough to pay the police to be his protection. Even if the case ends up in court, hackers often receive probation sentences because they can simply buy the courts.

BadB epitomized the hustling bandit-on-the-make. He had always been very creative: he was constantly coming up with out-of-the-box marketing strategies to stir up hype around himself to sell more stolen credit cards, dumps and other illegal stuff. However, sometimes he sold downright shit to his customers — his "don" status on CarderPlanet allowed him not to worry about his reputation. To be fair, a lot of us did this. It did not make us proud, but it increased our income. We never went as far as to sell the whole batch twice or three times, but sometimes we would sell dumps that were still valid if they hadn't been used by the first buyer for over six months.

BadB, as I later found out, was the same age as me, despite looking ten years older. A stout guy with brown eyes and two passports, Israeli and Ukrainian. Quick wits, fast mouth and long eye-lashes every girl would be jealous of. An easy-to-see ragged scar mutilated his upper lip.

"Vladislav," he introduced himself while we were drinking to finally meeting in person at one of the numerous night clubs in Moscow. "I grew up in Ukraine, now I live in Moscow. Once I'm bored of it, I'll go somewhere else. But so far I like it here. Everything nice that appears in the world soon appears in Moscow. Night clubs are the trendiest, malls are the size of a small town, any booze or drugs you might want, cars and restaurants are the best. Then again, Moscow chicks are the hottest…"

"How come you got an Israeli passport?" I changed the topic.

"There are ways, my friend."

BadB's last name was Khorokhorin. He was born and raised in Donetsk. Very emotional, impulsive and unreliable. Unprincipled, but very risky, with a great hunch for money — he hasn't missed a serious carding scheme anywhere in the world. Very communicative, a real gangster. The United States' enemy. His ability to be a jack of all illegal trades made him most dangerous: he did a bit of carding, a bit of hacking, a bit of spamming, a bit of forgery and, of course, a lot of worldwide adventurism. In the not-so-rare times Vladislav was out of money due to his habit of blowing it all on casinos, booze and hookers, he could always come up with a scheme that'd leave him with a couple thousands in profit in a matter of a few days.

He was fond of gestures like giving $20 to a kiosk vendor who gave him a glass of water or taking home all the strip dancers from a night club because we happened to like them all. Like many carders, he didn't have strong bonds to a single place of residence, his adventurous nature demanded daily risky shenanigans, so when I told him I might be moving to Kyiv for good in a week's time, Vladislav volunteered to go with me. He even booked two business class tickets.

I was finishing packing, BadB was waiting for me in a taxi. I still had to check my WebMoney wallet to make sure the $9600 I had in cash to give away upon arrival in Kyiv was still there. However, when I launched WebMoney Keeper, it didn't show me the money. I restarted the application a few times hoping for it to be just a glitch, but all in vain. Vladislav kept calling me every two minutes to yell about how late we were. I slammed the laptop shut, grabbed my bag and ran out of the house. Needless to say, we ended up missing the flight and buying the tickets for the next one, economy class this time.

"A drink?" BadB offered as soon as the plane's gained enough altitude.

"I don't really feel like it," I refused. "I've got a problem."

"What problems can a fine young man like yourself have?"

"My WebMoney got stolen. And I was supposed to give it away as soon as I arrive."

"Shit. How much money?"

"Enough, almost $10,000. That's what was taking me so long. The wallets weren't there. I thought it was a glitch, but nothing changed after I restarted the program. I guess I've been robbed."

"No shit, Sherlock!" Vladislav had no issue with tormenting me. "When a hacker gets access to a wallet, he doesn't sit there staring at five-digit numbers with tender eyes. He transfers the money into his Keeper as quickly as possible, then he immediately cashes it through the nearest cashing point or any other way available. It literally takes minutes. And it's almost impossible to ever get your money back. Every minute counts, so as soon as you arrive in Kyiv, get onto your laptop first thing, you understand me?"

Of course, I understood him. You don't just sit around after losing that much money. As soon as I got to Kyiv, I sent an email to WebMoney support, describing how my digital money went missing and asking them to do something about it as soon as possible. To WebMoney's credit, I didn't have to wait long for their reply. I was informed that $300 had already been spent, and there was no way to get it back. However, the remaining $9300 had been blocked on the wallets the intruder transferred it to. Also, the email contained IP-addresses of the thief, who turned out to be from Krasnodar. I should say I was lucky: it was now only a matter of time for me to get my $9,300 back, and the $300 stolen I accepted as a small penalty for my computer's security flaws.

"Do you want to know how you got hacked?" BadB asked after he'd finished two days spree of digging into SecurityLab.ru and other digital security portals.

"Tell me."

"Through a flaw in RPC DCOM, a service responsible for remote code execution. Have you received messages about memory errors lately?"

I nodded.

"What about shutdown of svchost.exe with subsequent computer restarting?"

"Yes."

"They got you too! RPC (Remote Procedure Call) is a protocol that allows a computer to run any code remotely on another computer, that's called Remote Code Execution. The hacker can run a code under SYSTEM rights on the victim's computer, which means he can do anything, including installing programs, deleting data, creating a new user with administrator's rights and so on." Vladislav was reading aloud the info he found on SecurityLab. "Computers with Windows 2000/XP and 135, 139, 445 or 593 open ports are all exposed to this danger. That's enough to break into computers of half the Internet users," he concluded, rubbing his hands in contentment. "Wait, when were you hacked?"

"Three days ago, 13th July."

"Right, and the vulnerability was only detected on 16th July. So, there's the rub!" my friend raised his finger, which gave him a resemblance to Archimedes. "It is called the zero-day vulnerability. That is a vulnerability that already has a code written to exploit it, but the program's developer either doesn't know about it yet, or hasn't managed to patch it up. It's immensely difficult to find such security flaws, and they also have sort of an expiry date — you've got to use them before they're fixed or blocked some other way, so exploits (malware designed to exploit software vulnerabilities on a remote computer) may sell for up to $250,000 on the black market. They're purchased by hackers and some countries' governments (to use in cyber war, for example)."

I got my money back two weeks later. I found a home address, phone number and a list of people, registered in the flat the hacker operated from. However, it didn't do much good to call — a woman old enough to have seen Lenin alive picked up the phone. Among the other registered dwellers of the apartment was an old man and a 12-year-old boy called Nikita. Could that brat have stolen my money? It was hard to believe, but two months after this while I was going through an old email that I hadn't used for about six months, I found an email saying the following:

> *I'm sorry I took your WebMoney. I know there was a lot of money, and you are going to look for me. I'm attaching ID, password and key for the wallet where I transferred your money. Again, I am sorry.*

Needless to say I was astonished. Had I read this email earlier, I wouldn't have had to write to WebMoney support and wouldn't have had my money blocked for a fortnight. I guess that little boy had actually broken into my computer. A more experienced hacker would have cashed my WebMoney in an hour and certainly wouldn't have let me get his IP address.

For a whole month, BadB had a hell of a time in Kyiv, attending all the bars, strip clubs and nightclubs possible. Then BadB went to Donetsk.

CHAPTER 14

CELLMATES

Cell No. 97 was situated on the fourth floor of the "old" cell block and appealed to me from the very beginning. It was about three times larger than my previous room, it contained 16 bunk beds, a massive (by the prison's standards) window and not that many people, only… twenty-five inmates.

I was soon treated to a cup of chifir, we drank to meeting each other and the usual small talk mostly aimed at finding out where I was from and what good I could do for the cell. If I could draw, put together board games or look after the road?

I looked around. One thing I noticed right away: everybody in this huge cell was doing something. Some were making horses for the road, others were pressing bread through a closely woven fabric to get glue, and someone else was looking after the road.

Dmitry Baton looked after the cell. He was a smart, handsome guy from Brest. A 37-year-old car thief, who had stolen over 30 Audis and BMWs.

"Well, hacker, meet your cellmates," Baton pointed at a bearded guy not more than 160cm tall, "this is Vyacheslav Beloskursky, he's also from Minsk. First-degree burglary," he introduced one inmate. "The one sleeping in the corner is Andrey Filonov — or Fil — he's leaving for a camp soon, he got seven years for assault with intent to rob.

Except you know how little it takes to pass for assault. Technically, hitting someone in the face and taking their phone, or even their jacket, would be enough."

Before getting into prison, Baton was known as Dmitry Batov and is the grand-nephew of a Second World War hero. I turned around to look at the man he'd just told me about. Fil had woken up and was now sitting on the bed and smoking a pipe. He was a little over thirty, had regular face features, glasses and a van Dyke beard.

"He's 34," Baton told me. "19 of them he spent behind the bars."

I looked at Dmitry in surprise — the last thing Fil resembled was a prison native.

"Moderately smart, devilishly cunning," Baton continued. "In a different time and a different country, he could be running some bank's security service. That fair-haired intellectual," Dmitry pointed at a tall skinny man probably about 35, "is Boris Chunosov, an 'illegal entrepreneur', facing up to seven years. He imported Nivea cosmetics into Belarus. Except them," Baton waved towards Vyacheslav Baton waved towards Vyacheslav, Fil and Boris, "there are a few good guys in the cell — they look after the road, despite being junkies."

Dmitry decided to elaborate. "Some junkies shoot stuff up for years without bothering anyone. Then the cops find out, send a rat to pretend to be a fellow addict and ask to buy a spare gram the next time the guy visits his dealer. The junkie agrees, partly out of good heart, partly to shave some off that gram. Then cops catch him red-handed. It's called a controlled purchase. Once that's happened a few times, you're looking at drug distribution, which is eight years at the very least."

"Those dealers pay them. And keep selling the drugs the cops bring them."

"Does he look like a drug dealer? Just a sick man that agreed to help someone he thought was in the same boat. And for the cops he's just a way to raise their crime detection rate — that's how they discover whole syndicates, bonuses and new stars on the shoulder boards for everyone involved," Dmitry kept on going.

"And how did Vyacheslav get here?" I asked.

"He was charged with burglary, including taking $600,000 out of the apartment of some presidential aide. The investigators really wanted to solve the case, so they forged the evidence. But Vyacheslav kept filing complaints and managed to shake it off. He was so happy he even confessed to a couple of crimes he hasn't committed just to get it over with. He's going to court one of these days to get his three years and head off to the camp. He's almost out of it."

"Say, Dmitry, why is he limping?" I nodded at Vyacheslav.

"He got beaten badly during the arrest. They deployed a whole counter-terrorism unit to get him. It's been four months and he still hasn't completely recovered. Ask him yourself. He'll tell you if he wants to."

The commotion in the cell didn't stop for moment. Everyone was cooking, smoking, playing or arguing with each other. We held conversations with three other cells (on our left and right and the one downstairs). All of that plus TV, radio and a large number of young people made my stay in this cell way more comfortable than my previous one. I blended into the team of Baton, Fil and Vyacheslav from day one: we shared food and cigarettes, worried about each other and lived as a moderately close prison family. About once a month I donated $200-300 for the cell's needs, and we were never short of anything.

CHAPTER 15

THE ASKING NEVER ENDS

Do you want to know what an interrogation looks like?

Your first questioning is like the first sexual experience — you look forward to it just as much, and you're definitely just as worried. You also never know when exactly it's going to happen — in the morning, afternoon, or even at night. You just wait for it nervously: you put on a brave face in front of your friends, but deep inside you're extremely anxious, because you know: this very first talk with the investigator may lift the veil of uncertainty that lies over your future. Even though you seem to be constantly expecting it to the point where you always keep a pen and a notepad at hand, the indifferent metallic voice that says, "Pavlovich, out! With your papers!" catches you off guard anyways. Your heart starts beating so hard you think it can be heard from other cells. But you put on a mask of apathy and go. Where are you going to? You're going to meet your destiny.

My first questioning took place on 4th October. You may say, "What the hell! You've spent over two weeks behind bars before your first questioning!" and you would be absolutely right. I was also fizzing with desire to find out what I was accused of. The detectives, however, don't feel the same way, and they have no problem with keeping you unaware of what's going on for up to three weeks. I guess it might be a way to put psychological pressure on people.

I enter the room and squint — my eyes have gotten unaccustomed to sunlight from spending time in a dark cell. Inside the room I find a shabby wooden desk with an ashtray screwed to it, a couple of stools also attached to the floor, a small window covered with a metal bar painted white, my lawyer and Makarevich, the investigator I was already familiar with, so lanky he looked like a pine pole. Thin, freshly washed hair, a cheap suit with trousers that obviously were too short… How old is this guy? I'm trying to guess, but the youthful ruddiness of his cheeks spoils my applecart as I realize he might be 25 just as well as he might be in his early 30s.

"Well, hello, Sergey," the investigator reached out to shake my hand. "How are you doing?"

"Thank you for asking," I shake his hand. "I'm listening."

"Here's the text of the accusation, read it. Don't worry too much about it — it's just a preliminary version and it'll get changed a few times over the course of investigation. Ready?"

"Yes."

"Do you admit your guilt?"

"I don't."

"Alright, I shall write that down. Sign here and here. Are you still sure you won't tell us the passwords for your hard drives?"

"You guessed it."

"As you wish. See you later," Makarevich rose from his seat and was ready to leave.

"When will we speak next?"

"According to law, the preliminary investigation takes two months.

That is, if we don't prolong it. So basically, any day. Good bye, Sergey."

"See you," I muttered under my breath.

I guess the fact they asked about the passwords means they still haven't accessed the hard drives. That's good news.

I went back to the cell and had dinner. The guys didn't bother me with questions. "Vyacheslav, tell me how you got caught," I asked Beloskursky to distract myself from my worries.

"They got me through the phones," I didn't expect him to be so eager to share his story. "I'd cleared out two flats nice and easy. Then I was calling the next one to find out the owners' schedule. I made the calls from a phone booth. One night I enter the flat, flip the switch, but the lights don't come on. I take out the flash light, turn it on and walk down the corridor. And suddenly out of nowhere I get a punch on the jaw. I fell down at once, from there I only saw dancing shadows, and they were all trying their best to kick me harder with their iron-plated boots, pricks. I thought they were ninjas, but it turned out it was the blasted special task unit. Where did I make a mistake? The phone booth card. I was changing the booths, but I never thought about the card. And of course, it had some kind of a system number. The cops took a printout of the incoming calls, saw the phone booth ones, checked the card number and looked up other flats I called with it. And I called that last one pretty frequently. Then they ambushed me. They hit me pretty hard, I think half my organs turned to mash," Vyacheslav gave a deep sigh and held his right side, "especially the kidneys. That did come in handy later, though. Helped me to negotiate with the cops, they agreed to take off some of the charges to avoid sending any of their boys behind bars for the treatment I received."

"So, Sergey," Makarevich addressed me with an inscrutable face during his next visit, "would you like to keep silent?"

"Yes," I answered without thinking.

"How about now?" he opened a notepad, took out a Parker fountain pen that must have been someone's present and wrote out the password to most of my encrypted hard drives deliberately slowly, like they do in cheap movies.

"Fuck!" I was stunned. "How did you open them?!"

"Very easy. You know The Bat, an email client? One of your brother's inboxes had the same password, and you know how easy it is to get a Bat password."

They now had databases of new and sold dumps, a list of my clients, information about thousands of Western Union transfers, all my accounting, scans of counterfeit passports, and, the worst part, a full history of my ICQ correspondence. Keeping it wasn't safe but it was also necessary for solving any disputes with clients.

"Damn, Dmitry! I'd strangle you with my bare hands!" I was cursing my brother's name.

"Oh, come on," the investigator didn't think my anger was justified. "You're not the first, and you won't be the last. So, are we keeping silence?"

"I will think about it."

"Take your time. See you in a week," Makarevich left with the proud air of a winner.

CHAPTER 16

A PROMISING YOUNG MAN

"Well, your investigator has really messed up the whole deal, hasn't he?" my lawyer said the next time we had a chance to speak. I couldn't tell if that was a question or a statement. "As I understand, there's plenty of evidence on those hard drives?"

I nodded.

"Until today we could have just denied everything and won — they didn't have anything on you except Voropayev, Batyuk and Saprykin's testimony. But now we'll have to work differently." Galina summed up.

"Is there any chance at all?" I was worried. "I really wouldn't like to spend fifteen years here."

"I understand," my lawyer sighed sympathetically. "Alright, don't be a chicken, I did spend twenty years in prosecution, after all. We'll figure something out," she added meaningfully.

"I keep wondering, how did you end up being a carder? Such a promising young man…"

The answer was a long one.

I was born in a village about 70 miles from Minsk, the capital of Belarus. For the first 6 years of my life, I lived in the village with my grandfather, grandmother and aunt. My mum divorced my dad when

I was just two months old. As I child I had an enviable memory and remember re-telling, in minute detail, the stories and poems my grandfather read me. My grandfather worked his whole life as a forester and loved hunting. My grandmother was an accountant for the local farm. Even aged 6, I was already a perfectionist. I remember drawing the animals from a book about Africa. I had drawn a nice animal, but the colouring pen strayed slightly from the lines — and immediately the drawing was in the bin.

In nursery, I was the only kid who didn't sleep during afternoon nap. I agreed with them that my favourite carer would read me stories instead. My mum came to visit us once a week, at the weekends. She was working in Minsk as a stock manager in a chemist's warehouse and lived in a hostel. When she took me to Minsk aged 6 so I could go to school, I missed my grandfather a lot. Every weekend we went to visit him and my grandmother — two hours on the train each way.

Grandfather was a holy figure in the family. He worked as a forester for 50 years. He loved everyone and you would never hear anything bad from him. He also loved his bees and making honey.

I was always a good student at school. I preferred the humanities, not maths or physics. I learnt English only when I started carding — because I was always talking by phone or online with dumps buyers from different countries.

When I was still a boy, my mother got to know a guy, who seemed to be alright but who, after they got married, turned out to be an incorrigible alcoholic. He was a former soldier and was good at earning money but he spent it all on drink so we lived very badly and only had enough money for food. But he didn't only drink. He used to bully and beat my mother and gave me a good hiding several times. I was always protecting her and never understood why we had to live with that bastard. Several times I had to spend the night with neighbors to hide from him.

CHAPTER 17

CARDERPLANET

Dmitry "Sript" Golubov, the founder of CarderPlanet

I guess in every person's life there are certain turning points. For me, CarderPlanet was one of those events. Of course, I was involved with stuff carding and was registered on Carder.org, the world's first carding forum, but 'Planet' changed everything.

I first heard about CarderPlanet.com back in 2002. I can't recall how, but I remember the impression it left. I must have felt what Ali Baba felt when he stumbled upon a cave full of treasures. Every section of the forum contained information on how to get terribly rich without leaving your desk. It was too big a temptation for a young man who could only hope for a monthly salary of $200 if he wanted to do things the legal way.

CarderPlanet was a unique source of information inhabited by carders that spent every waking hour there — it wasn't called a planet for nothing. It was a carder fraternity of sorts where everyone helped and supported each other. Aspiring to imitate mafia clans, the creators of the forum called each other "family". They were top of the pyramid. The family included Script — the founder of the forum, RyDen, Boa, Pan Kohones, VVC3, Bigbuyer and BadB. They all enjoyed trust and respect of the other users. All members of the "family" had "Don" statuses (Script's status was "Godfather"). "Capo di Capi" status users were responsible for safety and helped the "family". Despite the pathos that went along with the mafia-inspired statuses, Planet was a place of big hustle and big money. CarderPlanet forums sheltered all types of carders as well as hackers, spammers, computer virus writers and numerous other representatives of the cyber-crime world. Most of them were masters of their illegal craft.

Lots of unique and useful information, trusted people, an opportunity to buy all kinds of data (credit card numbers and paypal, eBay and bank accounts), safety (VPN, socks and proxy). Programs for spamming, selling counterfeit documents and bank cards provided a stable stream of newcomers. From time to time, people shared nice little trinkets for free. Planet gave carders everything they wanted: information, instruments and services. It's not surprising it became a home away from home for many of us.

At the time, I was a journalism student and was dating Katya — a fun, playful, witty and ambitious girl from a good family.

My specialty was Public Relations, something I was fairly interested in. Unfortunately, my mother's disastrous marriage to an alcoholic, constant fights caused by his drinking sprees, my lack of desire to live at home and a catastrophic lack of money didn't foster academic success. I spent day after day at computer clubs. At first, I mostly played Counter Strike — hostages, bombs, explosions, terrorists and counter-terrorists. We ate right there, by the computers, mostly instant noodles, chips and cheap beer. And when the clubs finally got Internet connection, I was lucky if I attended university a couple of times a week. Katya and I were on the rocks as well — I preferred to spend all my free time on CarderPlanet. What use was of journalism and PR if I could use my brains to raise $100-200 a day without stepping away from my desk! By the summer of 2002 carding had finally captured my imagination.

Once after another exam I just managed to pass, my friend Andrey, who doubled as my partner in small affairs on Planet suggested going to Cyprus for the summer. "A great idea!" I thought. "But the money is quite tough now. Alright, I'll figure something out." Still thinking about Cyprus, I opened a file with credit cards info that I'd had on my computer for ages. Other people's credit card info.

The first thing I got were the tickets. I used a card to book two tickets from Warsaw to Prague since they didn't have a direct flight to Larnaca. Then from Prague to Larnaca. When you book a flight online, you only get a digital booking and payment confirmation; you get the paper tickets at the airport upon presenting the confirmation and your passport.

Warsaw welcomed us with its modern skyscrapers — it was my first trip behind the "iron curtain". We got a $40 fine after penny-pinching Andrey decided to save money on buying tram tickets. We arrived at the airport and headed to the ticket office. Upon examining our passports and the printout from the website, the lady said everything was okay, but she would like to have a look at the credit card the tickets were booked with, or at least its scanned image.

"Shit!" Andrey muttered. "We haven't thought about this. What are we going to do?" he looked at me expectantly.

"We'll have to go to an Internet café and get that card scan. It'll take two hours at the very least."

"Ma'am," Andrey addressed the airport worker. "We'll have to contact the owner of the card, our friend, and ask him to fax us its scan. So, we'll pick up the tickets a little later." And off we went to the nearest Internet café.

"Andrey," I turned towards the computer next to mine and touched my friend's shoulder, "have you got any card templates?"

"Nope," Andrey answered dully.

I opened my ICQ contact list — none of my friends who were good at Photoshop were online. It looked like we couldn't create a scanned image of a card on our own.

"Sergey, what are we going to do?" Andrey asked.

"Let's rely on the human factor and go to the airport an hour before the flight — there'll be hordes of people at the ticket offices. And the cashiers will be tired after a day's work — they might forget about the card."

My estimation turned out to be completely justified, and we got our tickets without any problems. However, that wasn't the end of our troubles: at check-in we were informed we couldn't get on the plane without a Czech transit visa.

"But we aren't going to leave the Prague airport," I was using my best broken English to reason with the border control officer. "Here, we've got electronic tickets from Prague," I showed him a print out.

We were soon approached by an airline representative who saw we were having problems and came over to ask what the matter was. We explained the situation.

"Alright, guys, I'll try to help you," he said. "I'll call our company's representative in Prague, and if he can settle everything with the Czechs, you'll get your plane.

"Thank you," I was quick to express my gratitude.

However, forty minutes later he hadn't even managed to reach his colleague on the phone.

"Let's leave," I pulled on my friend's sleeve. "He's only pretending to help us. I guess it'd be bad for the company's image to give us a straight rejection, and he knows that."

"Yes," Andrey agreed, "wait a second." He headed off towards the ticket office where he asked for a refund to the card.

"Why did you do that?" I didn't quite understand what he was doing.

"Simple: if the victim notices the money lost, he'll look for it, and we've flashed our passports. But this way he won't bother much — who knows what banking mistake held some of his money for a while. Got it?"

I nodded.

We didn't go to Cyprus after all, not that day, nor any that followed. And that was a good thing. Why? Because it's a shitty idea to buy plane tickets with a stolen card. You flash your passport, the cameras see your face, and the time that passes between booking and the flight may be enough for the card holder to notice some of his money's gone. He may also make a phone call, and we will find the police waiting for us at our destination.

That evening we took a bus to Ukraine.

CHAPTER 18

LEVIAFAN

Odessa is one of those charming Ukrainian cities with its narrow streets paved with block stones, an air of provinciality, low prices compared to Minsk, and a relaxed way of life. Renting out a place in the midst of the holiday season proved to be impossible, and neither Andrey nor I had any friends in the city. We literally spent our first two days on the beach. In the afternoon, we swam in the Black Sea and sunbathed. In the evening, we boozed with the locals and wandered around the city. At night, we slept on the sand, thanks to the warm climate. Andrey was saving up for tickets again, so we walked everywhere. Deribasovskaya Street, Frantsuzsky Avenue, Grecheskaya Street. Odessa has captured a fraction of my soul, and I love coming back here again and again. The best time to visit is in early spring, when a wall of blooming plants strikes you with their splendor, and the absence of loud holiday makers brings the air of a millennia old power, and coolness back to the sea.

A good third of the founding fathers of CarderPlanet lived in Odessa, including Script himself. I had only worked with Leviafan, and since I happened to be in Odessa, I couldn't afford to miss out on the opportunity to meet him in real life.

"Hi, Phillip," I called up Leviafan. "I'm staying in Odessa, do you wanna hang out?"

"Oh, hi! Sure, my man," Phillip was talkative as always. "Where are you? I'll come pick you up."

"At the McDonald's by the station."

"Alright, man. I'll be there in twenty minutes."

Phillip's dad was a high ranker at the local tax office, so Leviafan, who turned out to be an errant, red-haired Jew aged about 30, wasn't afraid of anything.

"How come, Sergey?" an affable smile was dancing on Phillip's lips, and he seemed to scintillate with some sort of secret joy.

"By accident, really. We were going to Cyprus, got tickets with a fake card, but Polish border control wouldn't let us into the Czech Republic without a transit visa. So we ended up here."

"Where are you going next?" Leviafan asked, while ordering a round of cappuccinos.

"My buddy," I nodded towards Andrey, "is going home, to Minsk. And I'm heading south. We've been here for two days already. There wasn't anyone to stay with, so we were hanging out on the beach."

"You amaze me, man," Phillip shook his head. "You could have called."

"I only remembered about you today — so I called you. What is that?" I noticed something that looked very much like a Visa in my friend's hands.

"Oh, this… this is 'real plastic' from Boa. Have you read about it on Planet?"

"Of course. I've read everything on the forum. May I have a look?" I reached out for the card and took it carefully, as if it was made of glass.

"Don't mind the quality, there are better ones. However, it's good enough for shopping in former Soviet countries. When Boa came to Planet and spread the word about this new thing, our profits went up twenty times." Phillip rolled his eyes dreamily.

"By the way, why are they called 'Boa'?"

"It stands for 'Bank of America'…"

And that's how I first came across the thing that radically changed my ideas about carding, increased my income exponentially and became a dangerous, but profitable, occupation for the few years to come.

CHAPTER 19

INNOCENT UNTIL PROVEN GUILTY

The Russian city that I went to next was the home of my buddy Anatoly, who let me stay with him whenever I wanted. His stable Internet connection was vital for me and my empty pockets. I spent days studying priceless information on Planet and doing some stuff carding on the side. It wasn't even two weeks later that I had money again, which allowed me to go to night clubs and some of the numerous beach restaurants.

It turned out that Flint24, Carder.org's moderator, was also on vacation in the same town. We chatted on ICQ, met the same evening and were so happy to see each other we ended up drinking until 6 a.m. I was 19 and flattered I could talk with much older, more experienced and respected carders on an equal footing.

Alexey — Flint's real name — was about 30. He was a wise, calm and modest man. And his wallet was stuffed with Boa's fake cards.

"Look here, Sergey. This plastic," he took a card out of his wallet to show me while we were drinking German beer in his kitchen, "this one's from the first batch that Boa Factory made. It isn't very good quality — it's printed on a card printer, the hologram is glued so badly you can pick it off with your nail and the signature stripe is just printed on the card. It looks a bit like a real one, but the similarity isn't more than 50%. Here, have a look at a genuine one." Alexey got a real Visa Gold from some Moscow bank out of his pocket.

The card read "Alexey Stroganov".

"Alex, tell me, do you need these Boa cards at the moment?" I started working up to the question that was on my mind.

"Not really — I came here to relax, not to work. Why?"

"Can you lend them to me?" I blurted out. "It's a new thing for me, I really want to try it. If it works out — I'll pay you back and share the profit."

"Alright, take it," I was surprised by how easily Flint agreed. "But be careful: shopping with counterfeit cards is an extreme sport. It's something you have to be serious about, it's not a way to make easy money. It is a job: hard, stressful and dangerous," Alexey emphasized the last word. "There's no guarantee the POS terminal won't flash *Pick up* or *Duplicate transaction* (which happens when the actual cardholder purchases something in the States, and a minute later there's an authorization request from Russia). Keep in mind that you have to look the part. A twenty-year-old student wearing jeans (even designer jeans) and a T-shirt who uses a Visa Gold or an AmEx Platinum to buy a $10,000 watch looks suspicious to say the least. The first thing that comes to mind is that the kid simply mugged some rich fellow and took his card. Even if the cashier doesn't say anything, you'd better believe me he'll call up the bank to make sure he'll get his money. And who needs that? Who needs that extra attention and suspicion? Not us. The less you stand out the better. You also shouldn't run up to the most expensive item and scream that you want to buy it. The sellers aren't stupid: they are interested in letting you go with something as expensive as possible, and they'll offer it to you and convince you to buy it. It's less suspicious that way. Don't buy stuff right away, ask a few questions first. Ask them to pack it, and only after that you give the card to pay. Sometimes banks call straight after the transaction, and the shop assistant may be still packing your purchase. All in all, this is no walk in the park. And one last thing, Sergey," Alexey added after we'd finished the beer and were leaving the table. "Remember, manners are a thief's best weapon."

The next day Flint went back to Moscow, and I tried out one of his cards. I took great care in choosing my first shop: a quiet street, a small sports clothes store, no security guards and three shop assistants who didn't look like they could run fast. I picked out a pair of silver Nike shoes, went up to the register and handed over my Visa Classic to the cashier. She swiped it through the POS-terminal, punched in the purchase price, then there was a pause… then the POS started printing a receipt, which must be one of the best sounds in the world. A sigh of relief. I signed the receipt. Suddenly a second cashier with a pony tail appears out of nowhere,

"Sir, the signature on your card is really worn out."

"Well, the card isn't that new," I surprised myself with how quickly I reacted.

The answer seemed to have sufficed. A second sigh of relief. I took the shoes, the card and the cashiers said: "Have a nice day!" Yeh, a nice day to you too, girls.

My first experience was a success. I guess I could have carried on, but self-preservation told me a nineteen-year-old buying expensive stuff in bulk in a small town might look suspicious. Also, the euphoria from my first shopping trip wouldn't let me focus.

I returned home, and told Anatoly about my achievement. I also told him how to work with plastic and gave him the one card I had left.

The next morning, I had hardly got out of bed when Anatoly appeared in the doorway with heaps of various trophies and started telling me about his adventures. He was so excited he started stuttering,

"Sergey, I tried your Classic from yesterday — it was already blocked. But this card — he drew the other one I had given him out of his pocket — seems like it will last forever. Let's go."

I took a shower, we had a quick breakfast and embarked on a new shopping spree that resulted in a generous amount of gold, household appliances and super pricy designer clothes.

CHAPTER 20

WHEN A FRIEND LETS YOU DOWN

"Where did you meet your associates?" investigator Makarevich chose this question to kick off our next meeting a week later.

"What associates?" I was doing my best to look surprised.

"Oh, please, don't pretend you don't know them," Makarevich didn't have time for my acting. "I'm talking about Batyuk and Voropayev."

"I've no idea who they are."

"I repeat my question: where and under what circumstances did you meet Pavel Voropayev and Stepan Batyuk?"

"I've never heard those names before," I kept insisting.

"You got their pictures on your laptop!" the investigator was losing patience.

Shit, I forgot about the photographs. That's a good question: why would anyone in his right mind keep pictures of partners he hasn't kept in touch with? On a laptop used for all the illegal stuff! Another mistake…

"Alright, let's have a chat together with your friends and see if it'll help jog your memory," Makarevich said before leaving.

Six days later he summoned me again. My lawyer was already in the room. The investigator said something to a person behind the door, and a minute later Pavel Voropayev entered the room.

"Hi, Sergey," Pavel was obviously happy to see me and extended his hand for a handshake. I hesitatingly shook his dry hand and started examining his face as if to try and tell if I'd met him before.

"Do you recognize him now?" the investigator was watching me closely.

"Never seen him before."

"Alright," the investigator turned to my associate. "Pavel, who is this man?" he pointed at me.

"Sergey Pavlovich. He's the guy that made us buy goods at Minsk's stores," Voropayev said confidently.

It made me sick to hear it.

"Pavel, when did you two meet?" the investigator continued.

"In November 2002…"

I had to go through a similar act with Stepan, who was brought to the pre-trial detention center the next day to meet me.

"You're not helping yourself, Policedog," Makarevich spoke with what sounded like fatherly care, "the judges won't like you talking like that."

"And your wife might not like you fucking around like that, but you don't see me giving advice!" I snapped back.

"Alright, calm down," he said peaceably. "Have you seen this laptop before?"

I shot a glance at the Toshiba Satellite that stood on the desk with a printer connected to it.

"Never seen it before."

Makarevich smiled.

Of course, I recognized the laptop — it was my very first laptop, which Pavel and Stepan had bought with fake plastic in Poland. I later sold it to Nicron.

"By the way, how did you meet Nicron?" Makarevich seemed to read my mind.

"In 2002, on the Internet."

"Where exactly on the Internet?"

Right, you wish…

CHAPTER 21

FINDING NICRON

I found Nicron on Planet. Why "found"? At the time, I was considering rigging Internet auctions and was looking for suppliers of hacked eBay accounts. Nicron happened to be one of them.

A lot of people started off with auctions: this type of carding didn't require much knowledge or big investments (other than buying credit card numbers) and provided a nice profit when done correctly. The most widespread type of fraud on eBay has always been selling non-existent goods.

In short, the scheme is as follows: you get registered as a seller — for which you'll need a credit card. You punch in its number, and if everything is ok, the card gets charged $1. You use the same card to pay the fees for listing our goods for sale. You start with some smaller electronics, say a portable DVD player for $150. You can't start with something larger: eBay sorts all the products into different categories according by their appeal to fraudsters. So, if the very first thing you put up for sale is a camera, laptop or LED TV, your account will simply be closed.

The person who wins the auction will pay you via a cheque or a money order. You can also talk them into doing it via a wire transfer or using Western Union. In the meantime, you contact the cash mule and send him to cash the cheque. Sometimes it takes a few days. The victim will start complaining and saying he'll revoke the payment. To stall, you get the cash mule to send him something with the same weight as the purchase, a book or a brick, and give the victim the tracking number.

That will give you a couple of days.

The more positive feedback and reviews your account has the better: people put little trust in brand-new accounts. How do you get that? You can get all that positive feedback from fake buyers' accounts. You can hack into a website that's got information about other eBay accounts. But Nicron, however, hacked eBay itself.

Scorpo, Nicron's brother, was one of the best hackers in the world. At that time, he was the main dump provider for the international black market. I was a moderator of a few sections on LNCrew, a small carding forum, and for some time was selling Nicron's eBay accounts there and on Planet. However, selling them evoked numerous disputes so, little by little, I stopped doing it. Turned out that Nicron had loads of dumps, and selling them was way more profitable than selling the hacked auction accounts or credit card numbers that sold before I met Nicron. That's how I became a dumps seller.

CHAPTER 22

NICRON

"Who is Boris Drunkman?" Galina whispered to me when Makarevich left the room. "Is that the Nicron the investigator asked about?"

"Yes. But how do you know?"

"I checked with my people. Your associates have ratted him out as well. How did he end up in Minsk?"

March 2003 was a difficult month for Nicron. A mafia boss, Boris's close friend, was murdered in his own car. Boris was in the car when the killer ran up to it and unloaded a whole charger into the man. Before dying, the boss covered Boris with his body. One of the bullets did pass through and broke Boris's rib. It wasn't safe for him to stay at home in Russia's northern Komi Republic any more, and I invited him to Minsk. He took the offer right away.

Boris turned out to be an intelligent, sentimental, well-mannered man of my age. He was a fan of crooner Mikhail Krug and McDonald's. We rented a flat in the center of the city and from that moment I've never moved back in with my parents. Every day, Nicron hacked into websites and payment systems, and I sold dumps from the massive database that Nicron shared with his brother, Scorpo. Needless to say, we were never short of money. Together with Jungi (a Capo dei Capi from Planet) we were doing refunds. We hacked into online shops and charged a thousand credit cards a few dollars each. We then saved the money on one account and made a refund to one of Jungi's cards. He cashed it at ATMs and sent us our 50%. Later, Nicron taught me to use Fluxay scanner to look for vulnerabilities, and make SQL-injections, so I tried my hand at hacking. Small things, mostly — my skills weren't enough for a major hack.

"Do you happen to know where Nicron is at the moment?" Makarevich asked in a soft-spoken voice once he was back in the room.

"I don't," I said, despite knowing not only the city, but also the exact address of Boris's flat.

"I can tell you how he managed to get away," Makarevich was trying his best to get me interested.

"Save it. Boris told me."

"So, I was leaving the house," I could remember Nicron's story as if I heard it only yesterday, "and saw the cops were waiting on the stairs. I recalled my army training: kicked one in the balls and hit the other in the neck with the sharp of my hand. I ran out of the building, jumped into the car and hit the gas. I drove around the corner, grabbed my laptop and encoder from Natasha, blew her a goodbye kiss and headed to Russia. I'm done with your Belarus."

"Well, that isn't exactly what happened," Makarevich responded. "It was a mistake on our officers' part: they were waiting for him by the building, so he simply walked out of the door, got into his car, blocked the doors and drove off. Nearly ran over one of our guys. That's a nice story he put together with his army training, though, I'll give him that."

"Does it really matter? The point is the guy kept his cool — which gave him his freedom. It's like looking for a needle in a haystack now."

"You're right, it doesn't really matter now. Better tell me how you ended up in Kyiv."

CHAPTER 23

IN KYIV

In March 2003, Boa and Liratto (the masterminds of Boa Factory) were arrested in Cyprus and Russian counterfeit plastic manufacturers suffered their first major losses. This news was huge on CarderPlanet, and people willing to make quick money on someone else's big name quickly came forward. Soon, forums and inboxes filled up with spam offering fake passports and other services. All the offers contained Boa Factory in the address line and led to an exact copy of Boa's website — complete rip-offs.

Around the same time, I needed some equipment to make fake cards and I tried dialing Liratto's old number in the hope it would be picked up by one of Boa's employees who had evaded arrest. Surprisingly, someone answered. A man called Alexander told me how Boa and Liratto were seized by the police and asked who I was, what I was doing. They told me what they could do and left me with their contact details. In April, Alexander and his friend Sergey came to Minsk with the equipment I needed.

It wasn't even three months after Boa Factory got arrested that the police got Flint, Bigbuyer and Michael of RealPlastic.org. Gabrik, who sold them Nicron and Scorpo's dumps, was put on the international wanted list. Planet organized a fund raising for them: we all understood it could happen to any of us. I don't remember, how much money they managed to raise, but they definitely weren't short of sympathy.

A couple of days after Flint's office was busted I got a phone call from my mum. She told me our apartment had been searched. I didn't know the exact reason — it could have been anything, from my shopping sprees around Minsk with Pavel and Stepan to my connection with Flint. I decided not to tempt fate and headed first to Poland, and then to Ukraine.

CHAPTER 24

MY FIRST $100

"Sergey, what did the cops say?" Valeed, one of my Chechen cellmates, asked kindly when I got back to the cell.

"The situation is pretty shitty, brother. My associates are ratting me out. They've handed over me and my best partner. I'm not sure what to do next. I stick with denying everything for the time being."

"Try to negotiate with the cops. If they want money — give them money. If you don't have enough — borrow it. Freedom is more important than cash. You look like you can make more cash, anyways. How old are you?"

"Twenty-one."

"That's really young to end up here. How did you end up behind bars?"

"I discovered my talent for entrepreneurship early on. When I was five, I would pass off wood rosin for amber and trade it for things I needed: badges, batteries, fishing hooks, bullets, arrowheads. Who did I trade with? Village boys like myself, slightly older ones. They'd never seen amber in their lives anyway. Later, I started to collect metal for recycling — brass heating elements, copper wire, old power converters. That's how I earned my first $100. In the mid 1990s, life became much more fun. First, we were selling and reselling red mercury, that doesn't even exist. Then Zinger sewing machines — there was a rumor they were actually made of Nazi gold and just painted black. Everyone started looking for them. It was an interesting time. Later, I spent two months working as a manager at my stepfather's garage, but the bastard didn't pay me. That's how I got into criminal stuff."

"When an entrepreneur doesn't find a way to fulfill his talents, he becomes a criminal," Valeed said philosophically.

"That's very true."

"Why Internet crime, though?"

"I got my first PC when I was 12. Most kids that age only had a gaming console. I got Internet access soon after. I was in my element. Do you know what stuff carding is?"

The Chechen shook his head.

"There used to be very few online shops, and to buy something you simply needed to punch in your credit card number and the delivery address into a simple form. Once, around 1998, my brother and I were playing Quake online. Once we were bored with gaming, Dmitry started looking up music websites and I read news.

'Bro, have you got any cardboard?' Dmitry asked me once, when I was reading.

'I have. Why?'

'Share it, I want to buy an album.'

"What's 'cardboard'?" Valeed looked puzzled.

"To make an online purchase, you need a credit card's number, its expiry date, the cardholder's full name, and the three-digit code on the back of the card, which is used to check its authenticity. Among criminals, this is called 'cardboard'. I got it by accident: a friend of mine was looking to buy, I volunteered to help, and quickly found a seller.

It was the darkest, blackest market in Belarus at the time. At that time, the only technological advances the cops were familiar with were typewriters, and half of the officers didn't even know how to use those. You could buy 'cardboard' in bulk at about $1 a piece.

My brother typed something into a form on a website (he knew English better than me), wrote down the address of one of our friends for the delivery, and a week later an authentic concert DVD of Deep Purple was in our hands. That's how it all began.

In mid 1990s, nobody knew about credit card fraud. So, Internet shops were happy to accept non-existent credit cards, whose numbers we generated the same way banks generate numbers for authentic cards. The fraud only came to light at the end of the month, when the shops sent enquiries to charge the cards. It goes without saying, the cards couldn't get charged, as they simply did not exist. By the time American shops came to their senses and stopped carrying out orders from Russia and Eastern Europe without additional checks, some carders had already made a fortune.

Of course, we realized we weren't doing something completely legal, so we never ordered goods to our homes. Instead we used third parties, typically referred to as 'drops'. Most often they would be distant relatives or alcohol and drug addicts we knew. Very often they didn't even know.

Drops that cashed money from other people's credit cards were given a different nickname by the American media — money mules, or cash-out mules.

There were no set rules when choosing what to steal — we'd take anything. First and foremost, of course, it was computer parts, LCD screens and TVs, digital cameras, laptops and cell phones — goods that were rare in former Soviet countries, and, therefore, sold well. The hardest part was re-selling: Minsk companies quickly found out about their origin and would only pay 40% of the market price. However, even that was profitable.

In 1999, most American Internet shops stopped working with former Soviet countries altogether, and the few that didn't started paying careful attention to make sure the shipping address matched the billing address. Sometimes they asked for a scan of the credit card, which I had to draw in Photoshop. It was extremely important to set up the PC correctly from which you made orders from. You had to convince the store you actually were a rich John Smith from Nevada looking to buy a couple of laptops. You had to use an English set-up for Windows and make sure the time zone matched the country you were allegedly ordering from. The shop might be alarmed even if there's a Russian mode on your keyboard. You also had to use a proxy-server to conceal your actual IP-address. Preferably, so that your new IP-address matched the state, and, even better, the town of the card holder. It was still a problem, however: the Americans understood pretty well, that a person has reasons to use a proxy-server. What were they for if not to conceal your location? So, your proxy can match the state and all that, but the shop still won't buy it.

The human factor should also be taken in consideration: for example, Americans usually shop online either during their lunch break or from home after work. These are the hours Internet shops receive the most orders, so your order is less likely to draw attention from managers. You should also mind national holidays: orders, placed during the holidays, aren't processed until a few days later and that delay doesn't play into your hands. All this made the process of ordering stuff on American web stores even more complicated. So, I had to equip myself with a dictionary and venture to German, Spanish and French stores, that remained untroubled by the carding community until then.

That's when I got hooked on the Sotheby's auction. Sotheby's didn't sell mobile phones, computer parts, laptops or cameras but it did have heaps of jewelry, brand name watches and fine art. At Sotheby's you can add two credit cards as your payment options, and if one runs out of money, the auction house will charge the other one. One problem was, they didn't ship to Belarus, but I found a way around this — you just had to select Germany as your delivery destination, and then write Weissrussland (German for 'Belarus') a few times in the address field.

In the middle of 1999, the Belarusian carding community found out about Barnesandnoble.com, the largest online book and CD store. By the beginning of 2000, a massive warehouse consisting of a few airplane sheds was stuffed with parcels from B&N. And then the store started selling the first e-books! You could get one in Minsk for as little as $100 (their market price at the time was up to $400). Then we found a way to contact Moscow retailers, and simply flooded Barnes & Noble with our orders. That lasted over a year, and, by the most conservative estimate, the store suffered about $1.5 million in losses.

Once I got into a big fight with BuyMicro, a big Belarusian stuff carder. I was in the wrong, but didn't have the means to fix my mistake. BuyMicro called me on my home phone to throw around threats. At first, I took them seriously, but then I stopped — he looked like all bark, but no bite kind of guy. A month later I had completely forgotten the whole thing. Until one night I came back from university…

'There are flowers for you,' mum told me once I stepped into the flat.

'What flowers?' I was surprised to say the least.

'Have a look, they're on the balcony.'

They were, a bouquet of flowers. Splendid burgundy roses about three feet tall each — I've never seen such a big and beautiful bunch of flowers.

'Mum, how many are there?' I'd attempted to count the flowers myself, but lost count every time.

'Strange as it may be, there are exactly a hundred of them…'

They give an even number for a funeral! — not the most pleasant of ideas dawned upon me. Whose path have I crossed?! Right — BuyMicro! He definitely could afford a bouquet like that. Sergey, you have got into big trouble. You should find the money and apologize, and do it quick. If BuyMicro was sending flowers that cost more than I owed him as a warning, I was afraid to think what he was capable of.

'Mum, who brought them?'

'Some guy in a uniform. He said it was a delivery and asked me to sign something.'

'And where's the packaging? The paper, an invoice?'

'I threw away the packaging and there was no invoice. Just a card.'

'What card? Let me see!'

The card read, 'With best regards, Flowers.com.'

That was a relief. I ordered these very flowers about three weeks ago with someone else's credit card, and had completely forgotten about it.

At the end of the year we stumbled upon Fototechnika.de. Stupid Germans! They sent us 68,000 deutschmarks worth of cameras, and called the police when realized it was all a fraud. And in 2001, right after new laws were passed, raids began. Some were ratted out by their drops, someone got their phones tapped, and the cops also kept an eye on the customs officers and delivery men. About 30 carders were arrested and everyone was scared. The first sentence for carding was given in Minsk on 7th June 2001. For the first time, people were sentenced under the article 212 (credit card fraud)."

Valeed Agaev, who was listening to me carefully, looked interested.

"Does it still work?" he asked me. "I have a lot of Chechen friends around the world…"

"I can't tell for sure, Valeed. In 2002, shops stopped shipping if the billing address didn't match the shipping one, and it's really hard to convince a store you simply wanted to buy a present for a nephew that lives abroad. Of course, you can get online access to your credit card, and change the billing address online to your drop's (given he also lives in the States), also sign up a phone the shop can call and ask questions concerning your shipping — all in all, it's a lot of trouble."

"Sergey, I still don't understand where you get stolen credit cards."

"It's very simple. You just have to hack into an Internet shop, and take their client base. It has all the information you need."

"Do you mean you can't buy anything online today? I don't want my card info to get stolen."

"There is always risk. I suggest only shopping at big stores — they're way harder to hack to get the client base. Even better, get a different card for your online needs, a Visa Electron or a Maestro. And only have money on it when you want to buy something online."

CHAPTER 25

VIVE LA UKRAINE!

In August of 2003, Minsk became unsafe — Pavel and Stepan were frequently questioned and the police were closing in.

Ukraine was to me, a twenty-year-old with big ambition and the money to match, a real haven. I was on both the Belarusian (thanks to my associates) and an international wanted list (because of Anatoly's arrest). However, I led a peaceful life in the center of Kyiv and travelled all around Ukraine with my real Belarusian documents. How was this possible? Easy: information about people on international wanted lists doesn't get to local authorities all that fast, and often wanted criminals can travel around the world and cross borders without any problems, not even knowing how many people are interested in their whereabouts.

In September, my brother got deported from the United States and came to visit right away.

Dmitry had lived with an acquaintance of mine in Chicago for a bit, then he found Arkady on Planet. Arkady was a Russian carder from Voronezh who had been living in the States for a while. He was a certified dentist, but carding was his true calling. Also, as it later turned out, the FBI were very interested.

"Once I was at home alone," Dmitry told me in Kyiv. "Arkady had stepped outside for a bit and Olga, his wife, was at work. I heard some noises in the garage and went to check. In the garage, all I could see were officers — FBI, Secret Service, the local police. They gestured at me to keep silent — I guess so I didn't warn the others, but what's the point — they had surrounded the house anyway. They handcuffed me and searched the house. Then I was sent to prison, and stayed there for two weeks. Then another prison, also a federal one. Three more weeks there, then the immigration jail, then home."

"Was the food alright?"

"Yes. The Yankees are cool about that — they feed the prisoners the same as their military. I once saw a news report, Bush was having a lunch with soldiers in Iraq.

"What about clothes?"

"They make you change into a robe, orange, beige or blue, depends on the prison. You are transported in handcuffs and shackles, connected with a chain. I watched a lot of movies on DVD while I was there. There aren't mobile phones, but they've got loads of drugs: weed, ecstasy, cocaine — as long as you've got the cash."

"How long did they keep you?"

"A month and a half. Then the migration service workers took me to Warsaw. They made sure I got on a flight to Minsk, but didn't go with me. At the airport, I got a 'deported' stamp and a ten-year ban on entering the United States."

"What happened to Arkady?"

"He's in jail, but Olga said will soon get out and go to Russia."

"But why did they get you? I got a call from your mum one morning, she was crying and told me you got arrested in the States. Didn't tell me why or what happened. She said they could release you on bail, but we didn't have that kind of money."

"I had a few counterfeit credit cards in my bag. They figured I was an associate of Arkady's."

"I see. What next?"

"I told them they were Arkady's credit cards."

"What else could you say."

"What's that supposed to mean?" my brother took offence.

"Don't look at me like that. I meant, if they were after Arkady for a while, they were going to get him anyway, why both got to jail for the same thing? I guess it only made sense he took the rap for those cards on as well."

CHAPTER 26

RULES OF PRISON LIFE

I had been in jail for three months.

The routine was monotonous. In the morning, we went for a walk in the prison yard after breakfast. To be honest, it would be a gross overstatement to call it a yard — the largest wasn't bigger than an average living room, and the smallest was about the size of an elevator. A thick metal bar with a net thrown over it divided the skies into neat squares.

From time to time we watched TV. When we got bored of it, we played cards. The most popular games were Rams and Preferans. You could bribe the cops to get you cards, or make them yourself. You could get sent to a punishment cell if you were caught playing, but that didn't stop anyone. Officially, the jail allowed only chess, checkers, dominoes and backgammon.

"Just look at them," Valeed said looking around our cell one day. "They didn't give two damns about God when they were free. But now, when they've got innocent people's blood on their hands, they walk around with a bunch of crosses and icons on their necks. Seeing them believe in God makes you want to believe in Devil. Don't look for friends in jail, 99% of our cellmates are wolves in sheep's clothes, two-faced conformists.

Ask any experienced prisoner the first rule of surviving confinement — he'll tell you "Don't trust, don't fear, don't ask'. I would add, 'Don't blab, don't get in the way and don't hurry'. It is a closed system, and you have to have nerves of steel to remain friendly with the same person day after day. You always have to think before saying something. It's best to keep silent and look stupid than to open your mouth and let people see how stupid you are. Speak little and it will make people listen. It does much more good to know when to listen than to speak. Don't tell anyone your plans. You'll see people telling their cellmates they've got everything figured out with the judge and then be surprised when the judge is replaced. Don't give hurried promises — the best way to keep your word is not to give it. Don't insult or humiliate anyone, even people of lower status. Be particularly careful with sarcasm — a minute's pleasure from a caustic remark will be outweighed by the price you'll pay for it. Speaking without thinking is like shooting without aiming. Train yourself not to take anything close to heart. Don't let people get to you. I have seen grown men cry when their cellmates figured out how much they depended on letters from home and wrote fake ones from their wives saying they should break up."

"That is harsh," I imagined myself receiving a similar letter.

"That reminds me of an anecdote," my friend continued. "A soldier gets a letter from his girlfriend saying she met another guy and wants her pictures back. He sends her a bunch of photos with a note, 'Honey, I can't remember which one you are. Please, take your picture and send the rest back.' That's how you should act. Become a greasy ball that no one can hold or squeeze. Don't show anyone your weak points. Suppress all attempts to talk about your private life. There are plenty of guys in jail who would ask you about what you do with your missus, and then force you to join their own harem…"

"Wait, what?" I interrupted. I couldn't understand how anything you do with a woman could possibly be a reason to forcefully turn you into a passive homosexual. "What gets you in trouble?"

"Going down on your woman would. Or even kissing her after she did the same for you. Interesting detail is, most men don't mind doing things they will give you hell for, they just don't blab about it. People here pretend the sexual revolution never happened, and many prisoners in Russia become victims of sexual harassment. Try not to get in anyone's way. If you're not sure, what to do, consult a more experienced prisoner. If you haven't got any in your cell — send a note around the block — there must be someone somewhere. Avoid conflicts, try to respect yourself, others and the cell's routine. Don't get involved with other people's card games — not even if you see someone's cheating. Don't get into arguments. The only way to win in an argument is not to get involved. And the last thing, Sergcy: never take other's possessions without asking. You'll figure out the rest — don't be afraid and be yourself."

CHAPTER 27

DRUGS IN THE CAR

Misery loves company.

Katya got into a really unpleasant situation with the asshole with me in the temporary detention center who I asked to call her. He wheedled his way into her trust, said he'd be able to sneak a cell phone into the prison for me through a relative who worked there and then shook her down for $3,000. When, a week later I didn't get in touch and Katya demanded the money back, he planted five grams of weed in her car and called the cops.

"So, how's it going?" Radnenok, a plain, red-haired investigator who replaced Makarevich a few times, kicked off our conversation.

"Shit, but I am used to it. How may I help you?"

"Are you still in denial?"

"I am."

"Looks like your girlfriend is a junkie, which must be a bad surprise."

"What do you mean?" I tried to look surprised. In fact, I had heard the story from my lawyer the day before. I also knew the problem was already being solved.

"Yeh, they found drugs in her car," Radnenok continued in a

malignant tone. "We could help her, but you don't want to help us."

"Thank you, but I'll have to turn you down," I said between my teeth before blowing thick cigar smoke in the cop's face. My friends had sent me a couple of my favorites, and even in prison I showed off by smoking $50 cigars.

Katya was taken to court on drug possession charges that allow for up to a five-year prison sentence. She'd been kept in a temporary detention facility for a couple of days and things could have ended badly if it wasn't for her father's connections and her innocence. It took great efforts to dismiss the charges and start a case against the man who had planted the drugs.

CHAPTER 28

STEPFATHER

My investigation was running its course. Katya was very supportive, sometimes she wrote a few letters a day, and was in charge of communication with lawyers and sending care packages (hogs in prison lingo). The investigator allowed a two-hour visit during which we first talked about getting married. But neither of us wanted to do it while I was in pre-trial detention facility. We agreed to wait until my future became at least a little clearer, and then make wedding plans.

Meanwhile, my mother was trying to get a divorce from her alcoholic husband, the very idea of which he rejected.

"Who's Sergey Novikov?' Makarevich asked during one of our meetings.

"What Novikov?" I didn't understand who he was talking about at first.

"Your stepfather."

"Oh, that imbecile. What about him?"

"He called about a week after you got arrested. He somehow found me — I didn't even know the man. He introduced himself and said he could provide evidence against you. Took my men a while to drive out to his village to grab it, but when they arrived, Novikov was so drunk he could hardly speak. Gave us some floppy disk with 'traces of your crimes'. Demagnetized, as it later turned out."

"He is full of shit. Ruined my mother's life, now he's trying to get to me."

"Seek, and ye shall find," Makarevich said out of the blue.

"What do you mean?"

"Everyone finds what they're looking for, sooner or later. He told the KGB about you."

"What?!" I couldn't believe my own ears.

"How did you think we found you? Batyuk and Voropayev had paid their way out. Let's put it this way: your case was on hold once you disappeared and were on the international wanted list. Then it was put in cold storage. You came back from Ukraine and hung out in Belarus for six months not bothering to keep a low profile — you went out, had fun, and only got arrested six months later. Ever wondered how that happened? And we knew you were back in Belarus almost immediately after you returned."

The more Makarevich spoke, the better all the pieces of the puzzle fitted together.

"So, you wouldn't be sitting here in front of me if your stepfather hadn't come to the KGB and ratted you out. He told them you were back in Minsk and not hiding."

That explains why there were KGB officers during the arrest — another piece of jigsaw.

"Why would he do that to you?" the investigator's rhetorical question interrupted my reflections.

Why… Actually, why? I couldn't find a logical answer, but I had one for Makarevich.

"He didn't think it was his constant drinking and violence that estranged him from my mother. He believed it was me. He thought I was setting her up against him. A psycho. He did his military service in intelligence support. That's when he took to drinking."

I'm not sure how to explain it, but less than a week after that talk with Makarevich, my would-be father re-surfaced.

He was put in the cell next to mine facing murder charges. A fifty-year-old man without criminal record of any kind. As I've said before, God is not a sucker, he strikes a motherfucker when he sees one.

"Let's get him transferred to our cell," I tried to persuade Fil. "Talk to the cops, I'll pay. Then we'll decide what to do with the asshole."

Filonov arranged a meeting.

"Won't happen, Sergey," he told me an hour later. "I guess, your stepfather saw it coming and wrote a legal request not to put him in the same cell as you."

Too bad.

In the end, he got nine years for manslaughter, but only served four and a half.

CHAPTER 29

NEW YEAR PLANS

The cops were doing everything they could to make sure I wasn't going to get off. They split my charges into two cases: one for shopping with Pavel and Stepan and another one for selling dumps. It meant I was going to get two sentences and serve terms for both. Of course, Makarevich had an explanation at hand — why make my associates wait until the cops figure out all of my crimes?

There may have been other reasons. A former colleague, who quickly became just a witness, paid a visit to my mum and offered to help to dismiss charges on my second case for a bribe of $40,000. My mother, knowing what had happened to Katya, taped the whole conversation before politely declining. We still don't know if it was Vladimir's attempt to get some easy money or if he was acting on behalf of people from the police.

In the meantime, New Year was approaching in the pre-trial detention center. On New Year's Eve Andrey Filonov called me aside to ask an important question, "Do you wanna smoke?"

"Thanks, I got some," I took a pack of Marlboro out of my pocket.

"I wasn't talking about cigarettes. Let's smoke some weed: it just came in today," Fil unclenched his fist and produced a few buds. "Came all the way from Holland. Have you tried it?"

"Nah, I've been living in the woods." Despite Valeed's warning against sarcastic comments, I couldn't resist it. "How did you get it?"

"It's not hard to get anything in prison as long as you've got money."

"When do you want to do it?" I lowered my voice to a whisper.

"Why not now?"

"Let's do it later — what if I get summoned again?" I didn't know why I was resistant to the idea.

"Bro, chill, it's 6p.m., who's going to visit you? You lawyer has left…"

"Alright," I let him persuade me.

Preparations took about an hour. Fil took a pipe and a small brush to clean it off tobacco tar. I got a thimble that was black with ash and had a very strong and particular smell — I could tell it'd been used many times before — and proceeded to clean it with a needle. Then we used a few large towels to shut off our quarters — four bunk beds in the rear end of the cell by the window, where we slept. We were a small crowd: me, Baton, Fil, Vyacheslav the burglar and a couple more guys…

"Valeed, are you in?"

"Thanks, guys, but I'm not into that kind of stuff. I've also got one more prayer tonight. Vodka oranges came in today, I'd rather stick to alcohol," the Chechen said confidently.

"Suit yourself. Tell us if you change your mind. There's plenty of this stuff here," said Dmitry.

"Listen up, guys," Fil decided to start off with a word of advice. "The weed is really strong — I wouldn't hit it too hard if I were you. I've seen people who thought they've tried everything and nothing could really affect them, get so high they were ready to share any information with the cops or break out of the cell after a couple of puffs. Wait a couple of minutes after you hit it — see how it affects you. If you don't get enough — we can always take a little more."

"Bro, cut it out," Baton interrupted. "It isn't anyone's first time," he paused and looked at us, "not even anyone's second, I guess."

And we hit it off. We took a couple of hits and decided to take a break. It was good stuff. Once everyone got high, we started sharing stories: the good and the bad ones. We laughed and chatted. Remembered our lives before prison. Then took another hit. I got too high. I couldn't even speak, let alone get off a bed.

CHAPTER 30

NEW YEAR

There was a knock on the metal door. The guards usually knock on it with a metal key to get our attention.

"What is it?" Baton shouted.

"Pavlovich," we heard a few minutes later. "Out. And bring your documents."

"Sergey, it's for you," Dmitry said. "To the office."

"Shit! I knew I shouldn't have smoked."

"Just don't worry, man," Fil was trying to be reassuring.

It took me some effort to get changed, grab my documents, a pen and a couple of other things.

"Ready?" I heard from behind the door.

"Give me a couple of minutes," I was stalling for time.

"Sergey, wash your face with cold water," someone advised. "It'll make it easier."

I was escorted from the cell. My legs were stiff and hardly moving. Thoughts were buzzing through my head: who could it be? My lawyer? She's been here already today. The investigator? He's got better things to do on 31st December, I bet he's at home preparing dinner. Alright, whoever it is, I'll have to make it to the office first. Don't worry, Sergey, act natural, I kept telling myself.

The prison seemed to have died out. It was already dark, and the corridors were only lit with "night" lights, all the inmates were preparing to celebrate the New Year — we kept hearing bursts of laughter from behind the doors we were passing. We went to the fourth floor, then the third, the second, the first, the second again — it was taking so long.

"Boss, what room are we going to?" I was trying to get a hint at who I was going to meet — rooms on one side were used for visits from lawyers, while the others were reserved for investigators.

The guard didn't reply. Silent as a fish. Could he be deaf? My heart was beating so hard I thought it was going to crash against my ribcage. I was escorted to the "glass", a tiny holding cell where you wait for a lawyer or investigator.

"Boss, come on, tell me the room number," I was hammering on the door.

"Wait a bit, you'll be called," came the irritated answer.

Called by whom? Called where? Another horde of humming thoughts. And then it dawned on me — the prison operative! What would he want from me? I guess someone has told them about the weed. What would he ask about? Possible questions started to flash through my head as well as answers that would best suit them. Jesus, why am I so unlucky? Why did I have to have a smoke? The last thing I need is a drug case being added to my sentence. What if this was somebody's plan all along? Didn't Katya and Valeed tell me I couldn't trust anyone in jail? How will I look her in the eye…and my mum! Shit, why did I have to smoke?!

Clank of the metal lock. "Pavlovich, out!" "Where?" "Straight down the corridor."

I hadn't been to this part of the prison before. A corridor about ten meters long lined with upholstered doors on both sides.

I was walking carefully, minding every step — I still didn't know which door. I was looking at the floor as well to minimize the chances of anyone noticing I was high. Suddenly the third door on my right was flung open.

"Come in."

Inside was a desk that used to be lacquered, and a chair. It was quite dark, as there wasn't any kind of ceiling lamp. There were two cops — a fat captain with a glossy face and a snotty lieutenant aged about twenty-three.

"Take a seat," said the captain, pointing at the shabby chair.

The desk lamp cast its light directly into my face. There was definitely no way to hide the fact I've been smoking. If it wasn't for the lamp…

"How's it going, Sergey?" the captain started.

"Fine," I was doing my best to sound confident and not let my voice shake.

"Do you know why I summoned you?"

"No idea."

"I got an order from the prosecutor's office to question you," the captain began to unveil the mystery. "Did you bribe the traffic police?"

"Bribe?!"

"I don't really care, I'm no investigator. I'm just going to question you and pass on your answers, and other people will decide whether to start a case."

"Alright. Ask away."

"This year you were stopped on the Minsk-Gomel highway…"

I realized I was starting to forget the beginning of the question while the captain was still reading. Strong stuff.

"May I read the questions myself?" I tried to grab the paper from the cop's hand.

"Not so fast!" he snapped. "You can't read this. You must listen to me and answer."

"Okay, but could you make it a bit faster? It's New Year's Eve, and I've spent the whole day with lawyers and investigators."

"Alright, you may go. You'll be notified if the prosecution decides to open a case. They probably won't. Personally, I don't see that big of a deal here."

"Hopefully."

"Is everything alright at the cell?" they wouldn't let me go.

"It's alright. A good cell, good people."

"Would you like to cooperate?"

"What do you mean?"

"What the captain has just said," the lieutenant joined in the conversation, "we'd like you to tell us about everything that happens in the cell."

"No, thank you."

"Alright, you may go," the captain gave up.

That was close. Soon I was back in the cell. When it was almost midnight, we got a visit from the block guard — the officer who was responsible for making sure everyone was in place twice a day, in the morning and in the evening,

"Happy New Year, guys! Get out soon!"

"Thanks! And a Happy New Year to you too!" we answered discordantly.

Simple human warmth. Only seven words, but you don't expect to hear that in jail, which makes hearing it way nicer.

"Sergey, let's go hit it again," Vyacheslav was pulling on my sleeve.

"Nah, thanks. I think I'm good," I turned down the offer. "I'd rather join Valeed for oranges."

"Suit yourself."

I didn't smoke again that day. We lit candles. Spruce boughs came out of nowhere. That nostalgic smell, all the way from childhood. And I think everyone was thinking about the people waiting for him at home, about family, tangerines, Christmas trees and champagne on the table. About children, wives and mothers.

New Year in prison is something so wrong that it almost goes against the laws of nature. It was my first one, for one cellmate — his tenth, and for someone else — his twentieth. How many more will there be? Thinking about it made me so sad my eyes watered.

CHAPTER 31

TRIAL

A police carrier used to transport convicts in former Soviet countries

I went to court ready to be found guilty under article 212 of the Criminal Code, which allows for six to fifteen years of imprisonment.

Every trip to court is a serious test of your nerves. They wake you up early, at about five, but the chances are that you'll be awake already — thoughts of what you'll go through the following day as well as the prospect of facing your family will likely keep you up all night.

You hastily wash your face, try to do something about the trembling you have from being either cold or stressed out, have a quick breakfast and wait for the "Pavlovich, out!". You grab your mattress to leave it in storage (they don't care how many hearings you've got; the mattress has to be surrendered every time). You take your documents and go to the holding cell with twenty to thirty others.

Everything in prison begins and ends with the holding cell. You smoke half a pack of cigarettes, wait a couple of hours, hear prison news (mostly about other people's sentences), have senseless conversations or do crosswords. If you're really lucky, you might bump into your people who are a part of your case.

"Hey, Pavel," I was somewhat taken aback with surprise. I didn't expect to run into Pavel Voropayev on my very first trip to court.

"Hello, Sergey," he looked paler and thinner than when we last met.

"I've sent search notes around the block twice to find you."

"Our cells aren't connected," Voropayev explained.

"How are you getting on?"

"I am used to it," he replied in an indifferent tone.

"What do you think will happen?"

"I'm afraid to think about it. What about you?"

You and Stepan have such big mouths we're all looking at two sentences. Let's stick to one version, at least in court. Deal?"

"Alright," Voropayev agreed straightaway. Suspiciously easily.

At about 8 a.m. the cars arrived. Though, legally, you are innocent until proven guilty, they treat you like you are in the wrong. Even people who have done little harm — for example, accidentally hitting a jaywalker — are transported in handcuffs. Men also have to hold their arms behind their backs.

I heard a metal clank and a "Voropayev, out!"

"Pavel, remember the deal!" I tried to make myself heard over all the noise.

It's worth saying a few words about the cars that prisoners are transported in. It's a truck with no windows divided into three parts — the driver's, the guards' and the narrow cages people are put in. There's also a six-square meter cage where up to twenty people can be placed. There's almost no light, all body parts morph into one giant creature and you travel like sardines in a tin. The handcuffs clench tighter on every road bump.

We arrived at the courthouse and were taken in through the back door. I got placed into the tiny holding cell with a 'fur coat' on the walls. A fur coat is a large number of concrete bumps on the walls that are supposed to prevent you from leaning or writing anything on them. Of course, people write anyway, mostly their nickname, article, sentence and the judge's name. The prison architects must be a creative crowd. Take the desk in the cell. You can't sit at it because the bench is welded to the floor underneath it. There are plank beds made of wood with gaps sometimes as wide as your palm. You can't use the toilet without falling off it. The square washbasin is made from rusty sheet iron. The water closets are not separated from the rest of the cell in any way. As for the bunk beds, in Belarusian prisons the top bed is so low there's no way to sit on the bottom bed without leaning forward at an uncomfortable angle. The pinnacle of this stupidity are benches in the holding cells that are so narrow you can only fit half of your ass on them and have to put your feet on the wall opposite to give yourself some kind of balance.

This all is only bearable unless you get another prisoner in there to help you with waiting. What waiting? Sometimes you are delivered to the courthouse at 9 a.m., but your hearing won't start until 4 p.m., or later. Sometimes your morning hearing only takes as much as ten minutes, and you then have to wait until 5 p.m. for officers to pick you up. Or you can experience the same as what's happened to Baton.

"Guys, you won't believe what happened…" Baton told us once after he got back from a hearing.

"What happened?"

After arriving from the trial, we were taken to the furthest holding cell. We were there for a couple of hours, nothing unusual. It was time to get back to the cell, but nobody came to collect us. Ten minutes later the cops opened the door, and they were all wearing face masks."

"What face masks?" Boris asked.

"Special fucking unit masks," Baton spat angrily. They got to practice their batons on everyone who was in the holding cell."

"Why would they punch people in broad daylight for no reason?" I was confused. "It is the 21st century!"

"It's common practice in Belarus," Baton said. "There is going to be a hearing for the Morozov gang — a crime syndicate from Gomel, about fifty people. They are going to hold the hearing at the pre-trial detention center and are putting up a massive cage for the event. So, I figured the special unit are holding dress rehearsals by beating up random people. Just to practise, you know."

"Holy crap."

When you go to court for the first time, you worry about how your nearest and dearest will look at you, and what they'll feel. It makes you ashamed and uncomfortable. It makes you tremble.

You get escorted into the court room: the cage, the guards, the government issue furniture, the bright daylight that you have grown unaccustomed to, your family and close friends. They were all looking at me with warm, caring, empathetic eyes — there wasn't a single look of judgement, and I had been so worried. You sit in the cage like some kind of animal, with no one to help you — your lawyer is across the room from you. Even in Russia they let the lawyer sit next to the defendant to help.

"Pavel, remember our deal!" but he kept saying what he'd said before. The prosecution asked for three years for Batyuk and Voropayev and three and a half for me as the organizer. That sounded great! The sentence was supposed to be announced the next day. A sleepless night, red eyes, coffee, cigarettes, shaky hands. The judge seemed to be enjoying reading out the sentence as slowly as she could.

Voropayev and Batyuk got three years. I was sentenced to five years in a high-security prison.

CHAPTER 32

A COMPROMISE

"What the hell?" I asked my lawyer the next morning. "Why did they give me that much? The prosecution asked for three and a half, so I expected to get three and a half years maximum. Not five! Why would they give me more than what the prosecution asked?"

"Sergey, listen. You can hire another lawyer, that would make sense. But I've done everything I could," Galina was trying to explain herself. "If they gave you three — the prosecutor would likely protest and ask for a repeated hearing with a different judge, where you would likely get about eight years. But if they gave you more than the state prosecutor asked for, there's no reason to protest."

I had to admit there was some logic to her words.

"Alright, let's keep working. There's no good in changing horses in mid-race," I tempered justice with mercy.

After the arrest, the cops had stripped my car of all valuable belongings — they took my Chanel shades, a diode flash light, Trussardi Python perfume, discount cards to the city's best restaurants, a Mercedes door handle and Etro pants, all in all worth about $2,000. I guess the fact I was surrounded with so much expensive stuff impressed them so much they didn't even mind taking a half-empty perfume bottle. Also, my laptop contained about two hundred dumps with PINs and about $3,000 in WebMoney and E-gold. Where is all that now? Only God knows — the judge decided out laptops had to be destroyed...

A week later my sentence was shortened by one year under an amnesty.

At around the same time the investigation decided to continue the other case against me, the one connected with selling dumps and managing the DumpsMarket forum. Makarevich decided he was in a position to offer me a compromise: selling dumps, depending on the circumstances, could qualify as violation of either section 212 or section 222 of the Belarusian criminal code, which carried a much softer sentence.

"Alright, listen up," Makarevich jumped right into it. "We've got your laptops. You know perfectly well what sort of information they contain. It's only a matter of time until you're found guilty on all charges. But I don't feel like going over tens of thousands of pages of your correspondence with clients and sending legal assistance inquiries to multiple countries. You've already got your five years, so the case has lost some of its appeal."

"What exactly are you offering, then?"

"I can make sure you get article 222 — aiding and abetting in counterfeit credit cards production, which allows for a sentence of between three and ten years. Interested?"

"You bet!"

"I will also write to the prosecutor to mention the invaluable aid you have provided for the investigation that allowed us to uncover a whole criminal syndicate — you'll get five years tops. It's a good deal. But take your time. Talk to your lawyer, she's an experienced woman, she'll know what's good for you. If you agree, I will put together a list of questions, you can then take a week to think about the answers, then you plead guilty, I carry out a single questioning, a couple of inspections — pure formality — and we close the case."

"Alright, I will think about it."

I looked out of the window. It was spring 2005, I was in high spirits, and the offer was more than appealing.

"So, what do you think about it?" my lawyer asked once Makarevich left.

"Very tempting. But risky — it could all be a trick. Didn't you tell me I shouldn't trust a cop 99% of the time? You said they bluffed a lot."

"I did, but this is a little different. He came clean. You do realize he'll put together the evidence against you if you turn him down? I think it's worth taking the risk."

We decided to do it. However, since Makarevich couldn't give me any reason to trust him except his word, the wait between pleading guilty and my sentence was a stressful one.

"Let's look at the legal side of Makarevich's offer," Galina suggested after I agreed to cooperate. "What's the difference between 212 and 222?"

"You see, if I simply sell a card or a dump, that's article 222, but if I take the same card and actually buy something or cash it out at an ATM — that's credit card fraud, article 212."

"And what did you really do with the dumps?"

"I sold them."

"What for?"

"What do you mean, what for? My clients recorded the dumps onto plastic, gave the cards to their cash mules who bought stuff all around the world."

"So, you knew your customers would eventually use the dumps to steal?"

"Of course."

"No, dear, you didn't."

"What do you mean?"

"Simple," Galina decided to elaborate since I definitely wasn't getting it. "If you knew your dumps were going to be used for thievery, you'll go under article 212 anyways — as an associate in computer thievery. If the investigator doesn't make sure you do, the prosecutor will. So what do you say at the questioning?"

"I'm not so sure now. What do I say?"

"You say you just sold dumps over the Internet. You knew your customers were going to sell your dumps on to third parties. You didn't think your direct customers had any intention to record the dumps onto plastic and use it to break the law. Also, didn't you say that would require insanely expensive equipment? Did they tell you they had the said equipment? I don't think they did. Or at least you'll say they didn't. The bottom line is, you sold dumps for further retail."

"But that doesn't make sense. Someone was going to use them eventually."

"Yes, but that thought never crossed your mind. I know it makes little sense, but, legislation is a flexible thing. Also, if you plead guilty, the court is going to base the sentence on your version of the events. Unless someone can prove it's wrong. And I don't think anyone can in our case. Now let's return to the text of your charges. Tell me in your own words, what you're accused of."

"I manufactured 20 items of 'white plastic' with PIN-codes. I'm also charged with creating DumpsMarket, which was basically an online platform for people involved in stealing money from other people's credit cards, and using it to sell dumps that have cost the economy of the United States $15 million in losses."

"Is everything you said about DumpsMarket true?"

"Yes, Makarevich didn't lie about that."

"When did you create it?"

CHAPTER 33

DUMPSMARKET

The fall of 2003 saw me in Kyiv. I was never short of dumps, or money. Of course, I did run out of dumps from certain countries from time to time, so I had to buy them from Gabrik, Auger (who later changed his nickname to Twilight) and KLYKVA from Boa Factory. They were all sophisticated professionals.

It's worth mentioning that, at the time, selling dumps on carding forums was pretty much monopolized by the forums' owners, and finding new customers was a serious problem. That's when I first got the idea of creating my own forum, which I later called DumpsMarket. At first it was located on .com and .net domains, but my competitors sent millions of spam messages containing the following:

> "Welcome to dumpsmarket.com — a website with stolen credit cards, child pornography, fake documents and full information on every citizen of the USA!
>
> You can get fresh stolen dumps here: link
>
> For credit cards with CVV2 click here: link
>
> SSN number database here: link
>
> Contact: panther[757] ICQ 44007777",

People that received heaps of those emails complained to anti-spam services and I had to hastily register on .cn and .ws domains. I must admit, I would also use this trusted method of getting rid of competitors, and once even took down BadB.biz (I'm sorry, Vladislav).

"Where did you get the dumps?" Galina interrupted my reminiscence.

"When you sell dumps — just as any other goods — you can do it one of two ways. You can sell your own dumps and be a seller, or you can be a reseller and sell someone else's dumps. Most people resell dumps. Hackers that can get dumps, seldom take care of retail, and prefer to trust it to people with a more stable customer flow.

Dumps were a specialty of Russian hackers — Scorpo, nCux, Nicron, ViperSS and Aizek[797]."

"How did they get the dumps? Did they break into websites or something?"

"Breaking in isn't the hard part. The hard part is finding a place worth breaking into. It's difficult to hack into a merchant, and there's no guarantee it'll have dumps and not just credit card numbers. Processing centers are even harder. On the other hand, there are lots of POS-terminals, and they've got pretty bad protection — that's what you need to look for. Ideally, you should find a payment processing center of a large retail or hotel chain."

"Were you a seller or a reseller?"

"When I was selling Nicron's database, I was a seller. But mostly I resold other people's dumps."

"And did you hack into any websites?"

"No, I didn't know how to. I found places with dumps and let professionals do the job. They got the databases and we sorted the dumps by countries, BINs and launched them onto the market. Everything always went well for the first couple of months, but then the hackers developed a taste for big money, they got new wholesale buyers and the prices became too high, even for me. But the worst thing was it was increasingly difficult to make my partners work: they preferred booze, drugs and girls. I had to either spend days online waiting for them, or look for new hackers."

"So, if I've got it, you didn't hack into banks' websites and the worst they can charge you with is selling cards someone else stole?"

"Yes, that is right. I don't care what I sell: dumps, cards, passports, condoms, tractors… Except stuff like child porn and drugs, of course. Dumps are really lucrative, though."

"Did you have a lot of competition?"

"The biggest players were Script, BadB, Tron, diE, Gabrik and KLYKVA.

"How much did you make selling dumps?" my income seemed to occupy a lot of my lawyer's attention.

"The profitability was normally between 100% and 500%," I evaded giving a straight answer, "and very much depended on the quality of the tracks and the pickiness of my customers. American dumps made up about 80% of any database."

"Did you have any Russian dumps?"

"Very seldom: we made a point of staying away from citizens of former Soviet countries. Why? We felt bad for them. In the States they have insurance for bank deposits, but in Russia and Eastern Europe they won't leave you alone until they make sure you didn't steal the money from yourself. There are enough well-off westerners to go by. Call it being patriotic, if you will. I don't remember when we adopted the rule, but it was a rule everyone respected: never steal from your people."

"How many dumps did you normally sell a month?"

"Between 5,000 and 10,000. Hackers often came by copious amounts of information — Nicron alone had about one million tracks in his database. There was sometimes so many the market was on the verge of overflowing. And it didn't play into hands of dump sellers. Of course, we could keep trying to outrun each other by lowering prices, but we understood we needed a wiser solution. Flint came up with the idea of creating an international association of dump sellers (at the time, every single seller was Russian, which made the operation easier), working together — like a cartel — to inflate prices and increase our income."

"How did the customers pay you?"

"Via WebMoney, E-gold, a bank transfer or Western Union. Mostly, Western Union."

"What else did DumpsMarket sell?"

"Documents — driving licenses, IDs, passports — the same stuff Boa used to work with.

"What about the quality?"

"It was quite good. However, they didn't grant you the right of residence in the country, since the passports were, as you understand, issued by DumpsMarket, and not the countries in question. They were simply well-printed fakes."

When I created DumpsMarket, I tried to make sure it combined the best traits of Carder.org, Boa Factory and CarderPlanet — eye-catching design, multiple languages, simple navigation and professional moderators. I added a few tricks of my own — BIN search, a selection of best defense software and articles on every aspect of carding written by professionals.

When it came to promoting the forum, I followed my intuition: I sold dump batches at a fixed price, offered discounts and bonuses, used word-to-mouth advertising and arranged collaboration with Chinese credit card manufacturers — they gave clients massive discounts and the best counterfeit plastic they could find.

Since DumpsMarket got most of its foreign visitors from China, it made perfect sense to open a section solely in Chinese. God knows what they wrote there, but the moderator was a man I trusted — Michael Cheung Ho. He and his wife Lam, also known as Candy, were heads of an international criminal syndicate that used counterfeit credit cards to shop all over the world and they were directly connected with the Triad.

Sometimes I felt lonely — I made an absolute commitment to my work, smoked two packs of Marlboros a day, put on twenty pounds. My occupation demanded I kept a low profile and didn't look for new friends. I didn't look for girlfriends either. It's not surprising I only slept with expensive prostitutes at this time — my income meant I could afford the best.

CHAPTER 34

LORD, PROTECT ME FROM MY FRIENDS

In spring 2004, Auger left the world of dumps wholesale and Gabrik's databases were running short. At times, we couldn't satisfy the growing demand DumpsMarket users had for high-quality dumps at reasonable prices. The only person who didn't seem to have any problems was the omnipresent BadB who had an everlasting source of new dumps. Naturally, BadB was in no hurry to reveal his supplier's contacts, but after an intense search I managed to find the owner of the dumps — JonnyHell from Carder.org.

According to Jonny himself, he had got his database from Wal-Mart, and possessed over a million dumps. The retail chain was still covering up the fact of the information leak. Can you imagine the blow to Wal-Mart's reputation it would cause?

At first, JonnyHell wasn't enthusiastic about working together and lowering his prices to the level I needed. However, my lengthy experience of working with hackers allowed me to push the conditions I needed and we ended up working together until the day I got arrested. Our mutually profitable collaboration brought me $50,000 a month, and I only worked about three hours a day.

Alexander and Sergey, my friends from Kyiv, didn't know how

much I was making, but were suspicious my income exceeded theirs by far. And they didn't like it. I knew they were plotting something against me, but I didn't expect them to play that dirty.

I was living on one of the most prestigious streets in Kyiv. Once at about noon, while I was still asleep, Sergey called to ask what I was doing and let me know he was going to drop by in a couple of hours. I had enough time to sleep a little more, so I dozed off. The doorbell woke me up. I was still half asleep when I walked up to the door and looked into the peephole. The stairs were dark, which didn't surprise me — someone kept stealing the light bulbs.

"Who is it?" my voice was still a little woozy from the sleep.

"Downstairs neighbors," I heard from behind the door.

"What do you want?"

"There's water all over our ceiling coming from your flat!"

"What water?" at least I managed to understand that much. "This is the ground floor."

"Alright, Sergey, open the door," which I proceeded to do, somewhat mechanically. I guess my reasoning was, if they know my name, I must know them. This lapse of logic lasted only about a second, but it was enough for me to open the door to strangers — no one knew this address except Alexander, Sergey and Katya. Three people entered the flat, one of them showed me his police ID. They shook down my apartment top to bottom, looking for money, computer and other valuables. There was $29,000 in cash, $6,000 of which was right on the desk, by the laptop, the rest — in a pile of dirty clothes in the washing machine. I was going to send the money to Minsk the day before, but slept in and missed the train the mule was travelling on. I didn't even have the brains to store the money somewhere outside my apartment, though I knew full well something was being cooked up against me. Inexcusable negligence.

The cops — a major, a captain and a colonel — took my laptop, two cell phones, the $6,000, my detailed machine gun replica and left the flat. At least they didn't find the plastic — there were about two hundred Chinese Visa and AmEx dummies under the linoleum in one of the rooms.

"Look, old man, we got a dangerous criminal today," one of the cops told the old concierge, who looked our strange crowd up and down as we were leaving the building, "he was keeping a machine gun on his balcony."

"I would too," the man grumbled, "to keep scum like you away."

We got into a shabby Russian car waiting around the corner and were at the police station in a couple of minutes. It turned out to be just a few blocks away. We went up to an office on the fourth floor, where I was immediately attacked and beaten mercilessly. The cops then cuffed my hands between my legs and carried on, this time making sure I was stretching my legs as far apart as possible. Despite the horror, I managed to understand they were hitting me at only half of their strength and were trying to intimidate rather than cripple me. A phone call that the captain answered with "Yes, we got him. About six." only fastened the idea in my mind. I was sure Sergey was on the other end of the line.

The beating and the stretching didn't cease for a minute. I would stand, my forehead pressed against a lacquered Soviet wardrobe, almost doing the splits, about five minutes later my legs would feel numb, and I'd fall on my back, tightening the handcuffs even more under my own weight. The cops got a printout of my mobile phone calls out of a desk drawer with Alexander and Sergey's numbers circled in red ink and started to try to find out who the numbers belonged to.

"I've no idea, whose numbers those are," I insisted. "I get about 50 calls a day, you don't expect me to remember every single number?"

"Those are the numbers that call the most," objected the fat colonel, quite sensibly.

The torture continued. The cops began their favorite game of good and bad policeman: one kept beating me, and the other took me aside every once in a while to try to talk me into telling them everything about Alexander and Sergey.

"Do you know who your friends are?" the major, who remained uninvolved in the performance until now, tried to pressure me. "They are very bad people, they won't stop at anything. They won't think twice about getting you murdered."

I kept silent. Then the rogue cops took out a shabby Soviet gas mask with a closed air-valve and asked me if I wanted to play elephant. I'd heard about this fun game before and was aware I wasn't going to enjoy it. The cops inserted a lit strong cigarette into one of the holes of the mask before putting it onto my head. I started suffocating immediately and panic kicked in. I tried to get out of the mask, pulled my head to my knees and managed to pull the odious thing off my head.

"I've got a heart condition, you morons!" I shouted. "Get me killed here and you're in deep shit!" the outburst was followed with a punch in the jaw.

The cops threw me on the floor where the fat colonel sat on me with all his disgusting pig weight and hit me in the chest with his elbows a few times. Then they suggested I write a declaration and disclose everything I knew about Alexander and Sergey (whose nicknames, the cops informed me, were Gestapo and Figure). I refused. I was beaten again, and then taken into the room next door where there was a young investigator, who seemed to have adopted Heinrich Himmler as a role model. I spent another hour doing splits and listening to all kinds of sadistic bullshit.

I looked at the clock: I'd been at the station for over two hours now, and I was sick of this. I wrote another declaration that didn't have a word of truth to it, which only resulted in a series of punches in the kidneys. The cops started to threaten me with the phone game — they put a cord from an old Soviet phone over your ears and turn the dialer. The larger the number — the stronger the electric shock.

"Nobody ever got past the 8," one of the cops informed me kindly.

Fortunately, I didn't get the opportunity to try it first-hand, but I doubt it would have been an enjoyable experience. I re-wrote the declaration, adding the approximate number plates of Alexander's and Sergey's cars along with some other insignificant details. The whole thing still didn't contain as much as 10% truth, but it seemed to suffice. About twenty minutes later one of the cops got another phone call, and the bastards informed me that "serious people" had asked them to let me go."

I was picked up by Oleg, Alexander's assistant and driver, and I left the unhospitable building, relieved.

"Lord, protect me from my friends," I said with a sigh of relief, "I'll take care of the enemies."

"Was it that bad?" Oleg asked sympathetically, seeing my condition.

"Yeh..."

"Well, didn't I tell you? Friends make the best enemies — they know where to strike."

"You're right, I've given them too much information about myself — about being on the most-wanted list, and about what I was doing. You know, Oleg, I'm scared to think of what they'd do to me if I was really suspected of something serious, like a murder. I wouldn't have made it out of the building alive."

"Yeh, we've had cases of people jumping from the fourth floor because they couldn't stand the torture."

"They torture in Belarus too, of course. But not that often. The thing is, the police work by the Code of Criminal Procedure. And the prosecutors don't usually approve of such methods."

I never got back to my flat. Oleg took me to Alexander's country house. Sergey was also there, and they jumped at me, accusing me of not being careful enough. If it wasn't for a close friend, they said, who lived in the same building and just happened to see me being taken away, everything could have finished very tragically. Naturally, I was later moved to the idea of showing some gratitude towards my saviors. Buying them a brand-new $40,000 Toyota would do just fine. It made me sick listening to all of this.

My phones, money and apartment keys stayed with the police. Sergey realized I couldn't carry on working without them and brought me back everything except the keys and the money. I then stayed at a rented flat with 'their man' to supervise me.

Another mistake I made was using a fake passport in Kyiv, and keeping my real one at Sergey's place (because you shouldn't store documents with different names in one place). Now I realized that the most sensible thing to do would have been to keep all the documents, money and other valuables in a bank vault that only me and, say, my mum had access to. A week later, Sergey gave me my beloved blue passport back. Did my friends suspect I was going to get out of there? I think they did, but didn't want to believe it.

It took me about a week to win my guard's trust. He turned out to be quite a nice fellow, I even helped him out once by lending him $500. I took some of my belongings, called a taxi and left the city at night. Fidel had invited me to Odessa, but I went to Minsk, after checking with the right people to make sure I wasn't being looked for anymore.

I later found out Alexander was really mad at Sergey for pushing it too far with intimidating me, which led to them losing a regular income. However, it's worth learning some things from those two: they were both very serious about their safety. They believed a long meeting would inevitably fail, and never met for longer than half an hour. Whenever they had to attend a shoot-out, they arrived early and had a good look at the people present and noted possible ways to retreat. They always left their cars facing the road. Whenever we cashed out fake plastic, we made sure to acquire long hair wigs, hats and scarfs — eye-catching details people would look for. It was sometimes absurd — Alexander preferred to tap in a PIN-code with his knuckles as not to leave his fingerprints on the ATM. It goes without saying that we always left the cars a few blocks away from where we were going to 'work'. We also gave nicknames to places we frequented, so you could hear a dialogue along the lines of "Where are you?" "At the boards" (a bar that looked somewhat like a barrel). Or "at the base" (which stood for home). Paranoid, you say? It may be, but following all those rules made us almost invincible.

CHAPTER 35

JONNYHELL

Alexander Suvorov, a.k.a. JonnyHell

Before I got to Minsk I was met by Pavel and Stepan. They told me that even though the case against me was on hold, I shouldn't stay in Belarus. Unfortunately, I ignored them.

The summer was going nicely: DumpsMarket was pretty much self-sustainable, my alliance with JonnyHell was bringing me a lot of money and I wasn't looking for other sources of income. Katya had left for the States, I bought an E-class Mercedes, and together with my brother we spent the days driving around the city and having fun

— never working more than three hours a day.

One morning I got a call from JonnyHell, suggesting a meeting on a neutral territory — in Moscow.

"Come over, Policedog. It's about time we finally met in person, boozed and hung out with some chicks. Bring along friends, if you'd like — everything's on me," JonnyHell was persuasive.

I contacted Kaizer and invited him to join us. For the sake of completeness, JonnyHell dragged along a couple of porn stars from St. Petersburg.

"Where are you going?" asked a taxi driver at the station.

"To the President Hotel," I answered.

"That'll be two thousand rubles."

"Are you nuts? It's five hundred tops!" I was taken aback by such audacity.

"Well, the President Hotel isn't a cheap place. I think you can afford it," the driver muttered the last part under his breath.

"Not paying two thousand for a bloody taxi ride is exactly why I can afford it!"

I walked about two hundred meters from the station, and the first driver I flagged down took me to the hotel for eight hundred rubles. Kaizer arrived the following morning.

"Alexander," a young guy with fair hair and gray, slightly bulgy eyes spoke with a soft Baltic accent once I got down to the hall of our hotel.

"Sergey,' I shook JonnyHell's hand.

"Nice to meet you. Let's get some dinner?" he suggested.

"Where?" Moscow looked like a giant ant hill to me and I was really bad at navigating.

"To Red Square. There's a nice Czech restaurant nearby."

The restaurant was located on the bottom level of Okhotny Ryad, the shopping mall by Red Square — a mall with prices so high they boggled even my seasoned imagination.

The following day we met Kaizer who, to my great surprise, turned out to be just 17, and another guy from Minsk who was laundering Jonny's money via offshores. The four of us had a lot of fun hanging out with the pornstars in saunas, restaurants and even hotel rooms.

CHAPTER 36

SENTENCING

To Makarevich's credit, he kept his promise. Despite being on the opposite sides of the barricades and having no reasons to like him, I couldn't help respecting the investigator for his independence, and keeping his word.

I was judged by the same lady as last time. This time, taking into consideration all the mitigating factors, I couldn't get more than five years. The problem was that the final sentence could be partly composed of the two I was going to get. Also, Saprykin was changing his version of how he got the twenty white cards with PINs, and this wouldn't play into my hands.

"Defendant Pavlovich, where did you get the dumps with PIN-codes that you recorded onto 'white plastic' and gave to Mr. Saprykin?" the judge began. She was a stout lady in her early thirties.

"Your honor, I didn't record anything and didn't give Saprykin anything either. I didn't tell him any PIN-codes and definitely didn't ask him to cash out the cards."

"Mr. Saprykin claims it was the other way around," the prosecutor intervened. "How do you explain that?"

"Simple: he's lying. I'd like to draw your attention to his original statement after his arrest. He said I gave him the cards with PIN-codes and asked to get cash at the ATMs. He changed that version for the preliminary investigation and started saying I didn't give him any plastic, but left it in my jacket that I left in his car. And now he's saying he didn't even know whose cards they were, since they were in one of the jackets in the back seat of his car, and he isn't even sure, whose jacket it was. I've been claiming I had nothing to do with those cards all along. Also, the cards were in a pack of Winston cigarettes. And I smoke Marlboro. Ilya's the one who smokes Winston."

"Mr. Pavlovich, how can you explain the fact that your laptop's hard drive contained the same dumps and PIN-codes that were found on the cards that Mr. Saprykin had voluntarily provided to the investigation?" the judge asked, thinking she'd nailed me.

"I'm not denying selling dumps, some of them with PINs. Saprykin might well have purchased it from one of my customers."

"Witness," the prosecutor was addressing Ilya, "which version of your testimony should we take for consideration?"

"The first one: Pavlovich gave me the cards and asked to cash them out at ATMs," Saprykin muttered.

"He's lying!" I couldn't believe his nerve.

"I see," it was somewhat surprising the prosecutor was able to think straight for a change. "Your Honor," he addressed the judge, "I would like to appeal for a perjury charge against Ilya Saprykin."

"We'll address that later. Mr. Pavlovich, let's return to the question of how you came by the dumps with PIN-codes," the judge asked a very dangerous question.

"Your Honor, I bought them on the Internet. I don't remember, who sold them," I was spitting bullshit that people somehow believed.

"Do you know where your friend Mr. Drunkman is at the moment?" the judge asked, as if she'd just read my mind.

"I don't," I lied again, thinking happily that Nicron was safe now with his wife, kids and a legal job.

In the end, the prosecutor asked for a total sentence of eight years (he also asked to take the case in which Saprykin was accused of perjury as proven). Considering the unpredictability of the judge, who had given me five years when the prosecutor asked for three and a half, I was ready to hear "ten years."

But, fortunately, everything worked out for the best, and I only got one more year to the four I already had.

CHAPTER 37

THE PRICE OF FREEDOM

"Galina, they added another year, it's not great,' I was talking to my lawyer the following day. "I'd love to get rid of it. Then I'll only serve two and will be able to opt for a change of prison term — I've got this whole thing figured out."

"So, what are you suggesting?"

"Can you negotiate it with someone?"

She was back a week later. "I've arranged everything!" Galina was glowing with pride. "It will cost you this much." She passed me a piece of paper with "$20,000" written on it.

"Holy crap!" I blurted out. "Why so much? I heard it usually costs $1,000 a year."

"First of all, those prices are way outdated. Secondly, the papers are talking about you."

"I haven't got all the money. Half of it went to JonnyHell and Black Monarch who sold me dumps." I was trying to negotiate.

"Well, you know the price, it's up to you now. Let me know if you make up your mind, so we can appeal. By the way, why are the damage so massive? Did you really steal over $15 million?"

My lawyer was asking about my sentencing order, which said:

> *The guilt of the defendant is confirmed by written case materials: a statement from VISA Europe from 26 July 2005, which confirms that the 95 files stored on encrypted hard drives of portable personal computer of Pavlovich S.A., contained information about 22,452 bank plastic VISA cards, which were used alongside with 6532 cards, to commit fraud for an overall amount of $15,151,984.44.*

In fact, they could have chosen a higher figure — I've sold at least as many cards, I just didn't store all the info in my computer.

"Who exactly suffered the losses?" Galina inquired. "The cardholders?"

"No, the cardholders don't lose anything — all bank accounts in American and European banks are insured. I don't think they'll go broke — so I don't worry about them much. I don't get nightmares about my victims sleeping rough," I summed up. "By the way, what happened to my Mercedes?"

"Forfeited as the proceeds of your crime. At first the judge gave it to your aunt since she was the registered owner, but the prosecution insisted it was your car — they had the ICQ chat history to prove it. Yes, keeping those chat logs was a big mistake. Why would you keep them anyway?"

"I thought I could use them in disputes with clients."

"Well, there you go: someone else ended up using them. And that cost you $50,000," my lawyer was relishing this. "By the way, the license plate reads 9999TE, couldn't you think of anything simpler?"

I didn't answer.

"All your showing off, you want to be different so much," Galina was lashing me now. "Your car's license plate must be as unmemorable as possible — you never know when that will come in handy.

Alright, cheer up. It's just a piece of metal, you'll buy another one. Maybe next time you won't boast to all of your friends about how much you spent and blab about who the legal owner of the car."

CHAPTER 38

GREAT WITS BRING CASH OR TROUBLE

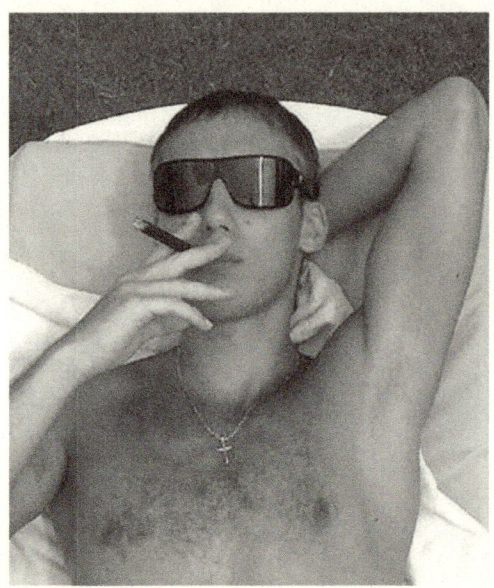

Ilya Saprykin, a.k.a. Postal

One morning I looked at the notes that had passed through our cell overnight and saw that an Ilya Saprykin was looking for someone. My oh my, was this the Ilya Saprykin I was so desperate to see? He wasn't looking for me.

"Andrey," I told Filonov, "it looks like the guy who owes me money is our neighbor. In fact, not only does he owe me $18,000, but he testified against me. Is there a way we could move him to our cell?"

"Let's try," Andrey agreed and set-up a meeting with the prison operative.

I was looking forward to hearing the results of their meeting the following day.

"It is the guy you're looking for," Andrey began, "his full name and date of birth match. The only problem is, he's at the hospital at the moment, trying to convince the doctors he's got a heart condition. It wasn't easy, but I've arranged everything — he'll be here after he's discharged."

A few days later Andrey himself got transferred — he chose a bad time to demand back money that a former customs officer in our cell owed him. The officer's brother turned out to be a big shot at the Belarusian National Police, and Andrey got moved on.

"Baton, one of these days a fellow is going to move in with us," I told another cellmate. "He owes me money. Fil and I arranged the whole thing. We have to secure him somehow."

"Sure, let's do it," Baton agreed.

"I don't know when exactly he's going to be here. I don't think anybody knows, except his doctor. But as soon as he gets here, I'll let you know and hide away somewhere — I really want listen to what he's got to say about me behind my back. Ask him about me — I'm sure he'll spill the beans. You know how it's done."

"Don't worry, pal, we'll figure it out."

Five days later the cell lock opened with a clang.

"Dmitry, it's him," I whispered and hid under a blanket.

"Good day, guys!" Ilya seemed to have learnt to present himself in the prison environment.

"Hello. Come over," Baton began. "Who do you happen to be?"

"My name's Ilya. I'm from Minsk."

"What are you here for?"

"Article 212."

"What's that?" Baton was trying his best to sound dim.

"Computer theft."

"What are you: a hacker or something?"

"Sort of," Saprykin hesitated.

"I think I know a guy that had the same article, met him here…" Dmitry was pretending he was trying to remember something. "You may know him. Name's Sergey, I think, his last name starts with a P."

"I do know him," Ilya lightened up. "He's in charge of food in the utilities block."

"Interesting. But that's not what I heard."

"No," Saprykin insisted, "I am sure."

"Don't you think you might be mistaken? I'm almost certain he wouldn't get involved with the food."

"I know what I'm talking about!" Ilya seemed fully convinced he was right.

"What if we find out you're lying? You know what happens to liars in prison?" Dmitry kept questioning Ilya's words.

Meanwhile, I was getting tired of lying under a thick blanket and listening to this dialogue, which was getting out of hand. I got out from under the covers, walked up behind Ilya and then abruptly sat down next to Dmitry and put my hand on Ilya's shoulder.

"Hello, my boy! Didn't expect to see me? Don't answer — I can see you didn't. What goes around, comes around, you know."

I sat there for a few minutes observing this man, who used to be close to me. I wouldn't call him a friend, but we had worked and had fun together. A man can say whatever he wants, but his true colors come out in his actions. And if words and actions don't match — stay away. Lies shouldn't be forgiven to anyone, especially friends. The problem is we love our friends and are often ready to turn a blind eye to their seemingly harmless lies. I let Ilya get away with too many things.

Ilya's voice had stopped shaking and his eyes remained the only thing that gave away the fear he'd just gone through. I returned to my bunk bed and called him over. I told him about what was going on in the cell, what he should and shouldn't do and assured him that nobody was going to harm him as long as I was there. I hadn't talked to anyone I knew back in my free days for ages.

"Ilya, I heard rumours you started working for the Computer Crime Department after I got arrested. That you were paid by them and ratted out a few people. But now you're sitting here in front of me. All this just doesn't fit. I want to hear what you've got to say."

"I was arrested by the same cops that got you. Makarevich was my investigator. All this time Artyom, my crime partner, and I were court-ordered not to leave the city, but as soon as the investigation started, they changed the pre-trial conditions."

"Why would they?"

"I wanted to emigrate to Spain. I was preparing the visa but the cops found out. That's how I ended up at the pre-trial detention center."

"Alright. I'd rather hear the reasons behind why you testified against me." I decided to get to the best part. "Couldn't you say the plastic belonged to one of the guys who had already left the country? Error32 or JonnyHell? I would have kept on denying it, and that would have been the end of it. They had fooled you bad!" I started to lose my temper.

"After they got us, I called my lawyer and he recommended blaming you to make sure we didn't classify as an organized crime group. To make it easier for you and everyone else," Ilya was telling bold, but convincing lies.

"Alright, never mind," I thought the conversation was running its course, "you're going to sleep over there," I pointed at a bed in the middle of the cell. Not the worst one, but kind of further off.

The next day Baton, with who I had become close friends, was transferred to a prison camp. A few more days later Ilya also moved out — I guess, his mother's money and pleas reached the prison authorities. I don't know, how he felt about it, but I wasn't too happy — it was nice having a friend in the cell, even a shitty friend. Also, he hadn't given me any kind of an IOU note.

If you are not familiar with the prison system, you might be wondering why I stayed at the pre-trial detention center and wasn't transferred to a proper prison camp. A man tries to do what's best for himself. At the moment of the sentence I'd been in Volodarka pre-trial detention center for 14 months, and I would be freed in a year to eighteen months. Also, I knew my way around Volodarka, and moving to a new place would be stressful.

So, how can you stay at a pre-trial detention center? There are several ways. You either join the utility unit, which means taking packages and books to the cells, handing out food, washing the dishes, cleaning the corridors and other rooms, doing the washing, cooking for all the inmates, doing small repairs. Or you have to get involved with "field work" — stay in a cell and be the eyes and ears of the guards. There are also people who have a formal agreement with the cops: this group, the smallest in number, consists of former businessmen, politicians, rich people and anyone else who has managed to negotiate a mutually profitable way of existence with the guards. This was the group I chose to join.

CHAPTER 39

FREEDOM

I didn't know the exact day I would be released until the last moment.

In 2006, a new form of incarceration was introduced — house arrest. It basically meant you could stay at home and go to work, but must stay at home during the night and at the weekends. I had applied for this two weeks earlier and was waiting painfully: who knows when the judge will have the time and will to go over my documents. So, when twenty lingering days later at about 4 p.m. an emotionless voice from behind the door said, "Pavlovich, out!", I wasn't ready for it. My mind went blurry. I got dressed, put a few books, post cards and letters that were important to me in a bag, drank tea, accepted congratulations — but I was doing all of it on auto-pilot.

The metal clank of the door and my heart started beating so fast and hard I thought its sound would be heard everywhere on the block, around the metal staircases, the corridors; it would bounce off the high arched ceiling and flies back into my chest. Ten unsteady steps, twenty, thirty, a hundred… the dark and shabby holding cell again, although in the light of new circumstances I see it differently. Another twenty minutes of waiting… the release certificate. I call my mum asking her to meet me, she says she can't, because she's alone at work and can't leave anyone in charge. The creak of the door closing behind my back... and freedom!

Your head doesn't go dizzy from all the fresh air and emotion, you don't actually feel anything particularly new or joyful. Almost immediately, your brain switches to more mundane tasks, and you start thinking where to get a taxi, where to go and what to tell people when you meet them. However, I still bear the heavy print of jail — I always try to keep a few meters' distance from people and I constantly think everyone is looking at me, even though deep down these people aren't looking at anyone — all they want is to get back to their cozy homes. Only after getting into a taxi to go to the pharmacy where my mum worked could I finally relax and look at my watch: it was Wednesday April 11th, 2007.

Later, the U.S secret service were very surprised to discover I managed to only serve two and a half years of the six to which I was sentenced. However, Belarusian law makes it perfectly possible: I got rid of one year thanks to an amnesty, and I only had to serve half of my remaining term before I could apply for early release.

My brother had been living in Kyiv for two years already, but by a fortunate coincidence happened to be in Minsk on the day I was released. When I called him, he was having lunch with my Katya. They came half an hour later. My mum was the only person crying tears of joy. We were drinking Martell XO from an old stash and didn't stop talking for a minute. Katya left. I thought we were going to see each other again later that night, but, apparently, she thought differently. I didn't insist and ended up drinking the night away with my brother. I remember going to have a look at the new National Library at 5 a.m. The following day Dmitry left and I called Katya again. We had a lot to say to each other, and I couldn't understand why she was refusing to meet. A few months before I got released I received a message saying Katya had been seen in the company of some guy. I didn't care about it that much then because I had faith in my girlfriend. However, when, a few days later she still hadn't found time or desire to see me, I started to doubt. At the same time, I didn't want to believe our relationship was a thing of the past and tried to find a logical explanation for her behaviour. I don't know what sort of internal struggle she was going through. She was probably asking herself if her love for me was as strong as when we first met. We did spend two and a half years apart. She was probably just waiting for me to do something. I don't know.

We only saw each other four days later. We went shopping — I had to buy new clothes and we decided to pop into a small café that we both liked and that was well suited for the conversation we had to have. We had some cake, drank a glass of wine each and made small talk. Neither of us had the guts to talk about what was really on our minds. Finally, Katya asked me directly what I thought about the future of our relationship.

"We could try to start over," she said, "but it's pointless unless you want it," she added, disappointed.

I don't know if she was ready for how things turned out, but everything that happened that day was entirely my fault. I was only thinking about myself. I couldn't possibly put myself in her shoes, and ended up pushing away a woman that was very close to me, crossing out two and a half years of her tears, expectations, hopes and worries.

What kind of person does it make you? — I ask myself today. A self-centered egoist, Sergey Pavlovich. I don't know, what would have happened had I not pushed Katya away that day, there isn't much room for guessing in history. We would have probably got married, had children and lived happily ever after. Wait 1 second — I catch myself thinking. You forgot to mention you'd keep cheating on her, you bastard. "You never deserved this woman, so life drove you apart," I think I hear a whisper from above…

CarderPlanet, the first carding forum in the world

ATM skimmers, devices that steal PIN code and data from your bank card's magnetic stripe

BadB with one of the first Teslas in Moscow

My brother and me, Barcelona Airport, 2004

Spain, 2004

Sergey "Fidel" Storchak, 2005

Gerasim "Gabrik" Selivanov, one of the largest dump sellers in the world

She was the first woman I was tryly in love with…

With DJ Aphrodite, the creator of Drum'n'Base, 2007

My brother and me, Egypt, 2008

Dmitry "Graph" Burak, Egypt, 2008

The Maldives, 2008

Same place, 2008

The food hatch in the cell door used to feed the inmates, pass letters, official documents and care packages

An average prison yard in a Belarussian detention center in XXI century

Stolypin, a railway carriage for transporting prisoners, on the inside

Vladislav "BadB" Khorokhorin in his prison cell, France, 2010

Roman "Boa" Vega at the present day

Today Dmitry "Script" Golubov is a member of the Ukrainian Parliament

Me in my cell with the first version of my book cover, penal colony No. 8, 2012

Same place, 2012

Me after release from prison, Icon night club, Moscow, 2016

CHAPTER 40

I REMEMBER THE TIME...

You can barely remember about having been in prison one week after leaving it, Kyiv, 2007

A man gets used to good things quickly. And very slowly — to bad things. And vice versa with memory. You forget bad things very quickly, and never forget the good things. A week later, I felt like prison had never happened.

Freedom gave me wings and the opportunity to do what I wanted, not what I was told to do. My life belonged to me.

Kaizer stopped working with me and, instead, took JonnyHell onboard to sell his dumps. To me he will always be a decent man. The fact that he returned $10,000 he owed me was yet another confirmation of that.

One person I no longer cared for was Fidel. He had promised to help me in one delicate matter — smuggling alcohol into a Muslim republic, but then backed out, switching off his mobile after I'd travelled 1,000 km and was some 20 km away from Odessa.

I took up tennis and was visiting a shooting club, where I could fire off up to 300 shells a day. I would spend hours on Mamba.ru, a dating website. I wasn't short of money — a bunch of people gave me the money they owed me, $90,000 in total, and I could easily have set up any business I wanted. But I wasn't in a rush to get back to work — I felt much more like catching up on everything I'd missed during two and a half years in jail.

I wanted everything, and I wanted to have it all at once. I took on a few projects that I had developed while still in jail: a spamming service, an Internet bank called cash2hands, a forum called carderLAB, and even my own premium vodka brands CARDER and HACKER. I only cared for dumps as long as they were one of the topics of the forum — I didn't plan to go back to selling them. I was really short of people I could delegate smaller task to, but I wasn't keen on the idea of inviting random people to work on my promising projects. Also, I was still spending most of my time chasing women, so these projects were taking even longer.

CHAPTER 41

THE TAIL

A few days after I got out of jail I arranged a meeting with Makarevich to collect a few files from my old laptops. The investigator was no longer an enthusiastic captain in ill-fitting pants: he had grown into a sophisticated major. I was sure he had been given the promotion for a few big cases, my own included. However, Makarevich assured me it was simply down to time served. We held no grudges.

Less than a week later I noticed I was being followed by at least six men in civilian clothes. To make things worse, I was sure they were making sure I'd notice them. That evening I received an email from Makarevich offering to arrange a meeting with "people who wanted to speak to me."

I called the number he gave me. A stranger's voice asked me to go to the Belarusian National Police. "When?" I tried to clarify. "Whenever you have time." "Alright. I'll come tomorrow."

At the entrance of the building I saw an intercom and dialed the familiar number.

"This is Sergey Pavlovich. I'm downstairs."

"Good. I'll be there in a moment."

The bespectacled person I saw next was none other than Miklashevich.

"Hello, Sergey. Haven't seen you for ages."

"I'd rather it stayed that way. How may I help you?"

"You haven't changed much," Miklashevich was followed by Novik, another officer who had taken part in my arrest back in 2004. "How have you been, Policedog?"

"Probably better than you. Can you tell your guys to leave me alone?"

"What guys?" he asked in fake surprise.

"As if you don't know. They chase me around the city, breathing down my neck. Identical trousers, short sleeve shirts, their radios going off at random…"

"Oh, that. That's not us. It's the KGB," Novik shot a meaningful glance towards the neighboring KGB building.

"You wouldn't notice a normal 'tail' that easily," Miklashevich joined the conversation. "But from what you said it looks like they were trying to get noticed. Let's go grab a coffee — we don't want to be chatting in the streets, do we? Do you have time?"

"I do."

I must admit hanging out with cops wasn't a normal occurrence, so I turned on the voice recorder on my phone before the meeting. Not the built-in standard one, but a program I had download earlier. Simply leave the phone on the table right in front of the other person and record as much as you like without it looking the tiniest bit suspicious.

We went into Myra Castle — a typical Soviet-style eatery where only teabags and mineral water didn't pose a danger to your health.

Speakers were blasting loud music, which neither I nor my voice recorder liked, but the cops seemed to feel differently.

"By the way, Saprykin ratted you out. If it wasn't for his testimony, we wouldn't have enough evidence to arrest you."

"Yeh, I knew that. That bitch…"

"You don't say," Novik continued. "He kept whining like a little girl, asking us not to lock him up. His dad — but I guess you know that — he's got a construction company."

I nodded.

"He owed my buddy $60,000. And wasn't going to give it back. He wouldn't return a dime until we put his son in a cell. Good thing we didn't have any reason to keep him there for too long. Didn't take his dad too long to give us $50,000 back. They're one hell of a family though — we never saw the remaining $10,000. Until we pressed his son again, that is."

"Why did you lock him up anyway? I thought you guys were getting along great."

"We thought so too. But when, even after your arrest, money kept being stolen from ATMs, we got suspicious. Do you want to know how Saprykin blew his cover?"

"Spill it!"

"One of the shops next door to an ATM he used happened to have a camera. We checked the tape and saw a black BMW. Guess what? The number plate matched Saprykin's elder brother's car's."

"What a moron! You should leave the car like a block away."

"We've got our people on every carding forum," Miklashevich was boasting now. "You'd be really surprised to find out who they are and what their ratings are."

"I'm getting harder to surprise."

We had been talking for about an hour now. I was still sipping the still water that my police friends had treated me to, Novik was telling yet another story — he turned out to be quite good at that.

"So, what's the deal with the KGB?" I was still curious about my possible surveillance.

"Right," Novik seemed to have awaken from something he was rolling around in his head. "The committee simply uses you, it cannot protect you. Or it doesn't want to."

"Can you?" I looked at the cops with interest.

"What are you doing now?" Novik changed the topic.

"I work in construction."

"As a director?"

"Nope. An assistant worker."

"Don't make me laugh! You, an assistant worker… Show me your hands!"

I didn't get what he was hinting at and presented my palms. Novik studied them for a few seconds.

"I see. Not a single callous. But you've got a Ferre jacket, a pricy phone and an even pricier watch."

I realized my mistake far too late: make sure to always dress your worst for the police, tax office and hospital.

"What do you really plan on doing?"

"I haven't decided yet. I've only been out for three weeks."

"If past experience is anything to go by, most people get back to what got them in jail in the first place."

"I'll still try to start a new life."

"There's no harm in trying," Novik kept mocking me. "By the way, who's selling dumps now?"

"I haven't seen any big bases on the Internet."

"That's because there aren't any big bases. There hasn't been since you left. Is anyone selling dumps at all?"

"I don't know, I'll have to check."

"That'd be great."

"Alright, I need to be going."

"Wait, let me finish."

"We've been talking over an hour already, and I still don't understand what you want from me," I knew the voice recorder in my phone was catching every word and I really wanted to hear their actual offer, which I could later turn into blackmail material. As if he'd read my thoughts, Miklashevich picked my phone off the table and pressed the on button. However, the only thing the phone showed him was a locked screen with no indication of what apps were running at the moment. Somewhat disappointed, he put the phone back.

"Give it a thought anyways," Novik said. "You are one of the best carders, and you behaved well during your arrest. You'll get back to your ways eventually. And, as I've already said, working alone…"

"Are you offering me protection or something?"

"Some things are best left unsaid," Novik finished on a poetic note.

Right. The Belarusian Computer Crime Department works in mysterious ways: intimidate a person with mock surveillance operation, blame the KGB for everything, and, finally, offer their "services".

That night I was thinking about what Novik said in bed. He was right about quite a few things. Even though I didn't like what he had to say about me, he had a point — the temptation to go back to carding was great. I saved the potential blackmail on my computer and left it there for better days.

CHAPTER 42

THE KING IS DEAD. LONG LIVE THE KING!

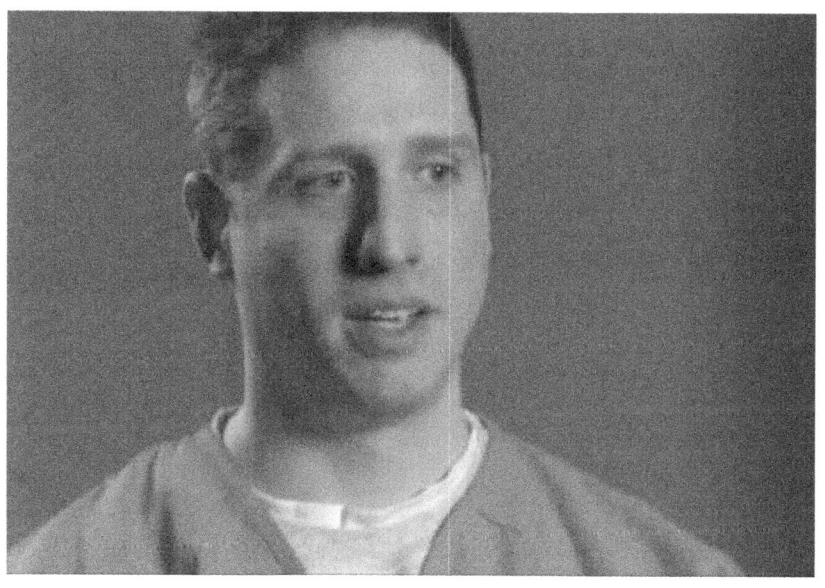

Max Ray Butler, a.k.a. Iceman

I started renting a flat in the center (before that I used to live in the suburbs with my mum), and my new girlfriend moved in with me.

I was honest with Irina from the start. About three months after we started dating I told her all about what I used to do and the fact I'd spent the past few years in jail.

"I knew about that," she surprised me.

"How?!"

"I knew from the very first day."

"Who told you?"

"I've got plenty of friends who are online. One of them saw us, thought your face looked familiar, did a little investigation and told me everything."

Goodness me, carders are everywhere!

But the community had problems while I was in jail. After CarderPlanet was closed down along with ShadowCrew, an English-speaking carding forum and about 21 of the most active members of the carding community were arrested, cybercriminals were frightened, disorganized and had no platform.

Of course, a whole number of new forums quickly rose from their ruins: theCC.ru, VendorsName.ws, StealthDivision, CardersArmy, TheftServices, but it wasn't clear who their owners were — likely cops and informers. English-speaking theGrifters was created with FBI money, and Verified.ru belonged to the Russian police. ScandinavianCarding, theVouched, TalkCash, DarkMarket.ws and the Russian-speaking CardingWorld.cc and Mazafaka were some of the few that seemed reliable. This continued until 2005 when a new big player appeared: CardersMarket.com, which, as it later turned out, belonged to Max Ray Butler (a.k.a. Iceman), one of the world's best hackers.

Max broke into the six of the main forums (TalkCash and ScandinavianCarding had no database backups and fell into oblivion forever), selected all English-speaking users (Russians didn't trust foreign forums) and forcefully imported them into his CardersMarket. Of course, this was condemned by the carding community, but a fact was a fact: CardersMarket with 6,000 unique users was now the largest carding forum in the world. It was bigger than ShadowCrew in its prime.

What do you think Iceman started doing as soon as he got his hands onto so many potential clients? Same thing as Script, Fidel and other forum owners, myself included, had done before him — selling dumps. In a short time, Butler became one of the top five sellers in the world — in a market traditionally dominated by Russians. He took certain precautions: Max created an alternative nickname to do the selling with. It was the keystone of his business strategy: Iceman, the face and the owner of the forum, kept his hands clean, while Digits, his alter-ego, was selling stolen magstripe data. Also, Max changed the way he communicated online, since he was afraid particular characteristic clichés and speech patterns could give him away…

CHAPTER 43

A CARDER-FIGHTER BECOMES... A CARDER

Cyber Crime Department Colonel Sergey Novik during his trial

"Sergey?" I heard down my phone one evening.

"Yes."

"This is the KGB speaking. Could you pay us a visit?"

Shit! What have I done this time? I asked myself and couldn't figure out the answer.

"Babe, is everything alright?" the puzzled look on my face seemed to have worried Irina. "Who was it?"

"The KGB."

"What do they want from you?"

"No idea. They wouldn't tell me over the phone, asked me to come over."

"It must be some kind of mistake. You don't do anything like that anymore, do you?" Irina was trying to comfort me (and herself). "If they lock you up, I'm not going to bring you care packages."

I guess I'll have to find someone who will, then — I thought discontentedly. But really, what does the KGB want from me? I'm not doing anything illegal although… I sold thirty dumps to guys from St. Petersburg, who owed me money. I'd also sold fifteen hundred dumps to Sonelao, a trusted client of mine. But none of that was enough to get the KGB's attention. Back in 2004 I could have sold more in a single day. No, that couldn't have been the reason. What, then? Fair enough, I was working on carderLAB, my new forum that was supposed to be better than DumpsMarket ever was. I had found archives of sites that no longer existed like ShadowCrew, StealthDivision, CarderPlanet and Carder.org, which remained a priceless source of information, and was planning to connect them to my forum — that would attract a lot of visitors. One thing I was definitely not going to do was carding. I wasn't working on my forum to sell dumps — I wanted to create a platform for carders and charge them for it. What was it the KGB wanted from me, then? It didn't help that my mum poured oil on to the fire by reminding me that back in 2004 I was arrested soon after buying a Mercedes and there I was again driving an expensive, new car.

"Alright, honey, don't get worked up about it," Irina gave my cheek a stroke. "I'm sure it's all just some stupid misunderstanding."

Irina volunteered to go with me. Well, she couldn't actually enter the building with me, but we arrived to the area a little ahead of time and had breakfast in a cafe nearby, still trying to guess why the KGB might be interested in me.

Turned out, we didn't have to worry. The KGB people informed me that one of the chief warriors against carding, my old police friend Colonel Novik (who had arrested me), had taken to carding and was now suspected of stealing money from people's bank cards.

That's news indeed — I couldn't help feeling excited. That was definitely worth a visit to the KGB.

CHAPTER 44

ADULT

I was spending almost all of my free time with Irina, only turning to work in the few hours she was studying or seeing friends.

Adult brought me money, but no joy. What is "Adult"? Simple — it's porn.

So, how do you start your very own porn business online? The standard scheme is uploading a selection of pictures and videos onto a site, selecting access options — usually it's something along the lines of a $2 two-day trial and a monthly pass for $50. You get connected to a billing company to process payments. All Internet shops use payment systems, but porn sites usually work with special billing companies, such as PayCom.

How do you get the pictures and videos? Webmasters usually buy the content from production studios — there are about thirty of them in Russia alone. A nice set (20-40 frames, one sexual act) will cost you $100-250. According to unwritten rules, the webmasters and the producers never interact in real life. Shooting porn doesn't always go well with the law. It's safer not to have connections.

The new owner then places the materials on a paid website. Its future consumer is a foreigner with a credit card.

A different, and more numerous, type of adult webmaster (AWM) are those that don't have their own content and who make money by attracting an audience to other people's paid websites (in AWM terminology they are "speeding up the traffic"). Usually they make complex systems of free webpages where every page has a couple of pictures and an invitation to a paid source. Websites pay their such agents up to $3,000 a month. There are thousands of such agents in Russia, and many more in the States. "Think about it," a friend of mine, a successful online porn seller used to say. "You get $2,000-3,000 a month for doing virtually nothing, and it's legal. The whole world either loves or doesn't mind us. This isn't carding, there are no victims, no police, no jail time. You aren't stealing anything — people pay for their entertainment, and everyone's happy."

There was infallible logic to his reasoning — and I wanted to try something new. That's how I traded carding for porn and became an AWM. Except I wasn't making $2,000, I was making ten times more. How? Spam was the key to everything.

CHAPTER 45

SPAM

Today, spam is 90% of all email messages. There is a low threshold to enter the business: it only cost me $250 to send 60 million junk emails. Of course, not all the messages reached their destination — filters, installed at most modern, free email servers, block up to 98% of spam. However, the mailing did bring in about 40,000 unique users, about 250 of whom bought a monthly pass to porn sites, which gave me an income of about $10,000. Domains, mailing fees, web-design services, hosting and databases of porn fans email addresses cost me about $2,500. Profitability exceeded 300%. Every month, I was sending out about 250 million advertisement emails.

Of course, it wasn't all that easy: first, I had to get the emails of people who were interested in pornography, since we had long passed the days when people got random messages. Today, spammers are way more advanced and prefer targeted mailings, aimed at a particular audience: Viagra and adult sites for porn lovers, an online casino invite for gamblers, and so on. This is why you had to buy and cherish your email base — it was one of your most precious assets. Who do you buy it from? Easy — hackers. My old connections in hacking circles made it easy. These guys broke into bases of large porn sites and sold the clients' emails, sometimes in bulk. I paid up to $1,000 for a million addresses. Sometimes I paid too much, sometimes I got invalid or inactive emails, but after some trial and error I arrived at the conclusion that it was only worth buying email databases with online access to the hacked source, which provided daily updates.

Another difficulty was finding high-quality hosting for my websites, since many users don't like receiving heaps of junk mail and they sometimes complain to services like SpamHaus, which kill off the hosting server quite promptly. Thus, a simple $15 a month hosting wouldn't do — we need something that won't go down with the first complaint. Where do we find such hosting? On spamming and hacking forums, of course! There are enough people on the Internet who will organize you a hosting space for whatever needs you might have. Do you want your own VPN? No problem, here's one already set up. Do you want a cheap hosting for a "fast" project which you don't mind shutting down after a couple of weeks? Here's one, for peanuts. Do you need a dedicated server that definitely won't get closed? Here's a private one in data centers of Turkey, Malaysia or China, where the owners don't care what kind of content is stored, and even promise to ignore any complains. It will cost you, though — starting at $1,000 a month. My hosting cost $400 a month.

However, that's not all. Anti-virus programs look for key words (such as Viagra or income), links and characteristic layouts to filter off spam. In response, spammers add extra letters, deliberate spelling errors and picture ads. That's how spammers break through the filters.

Various Internet projects use the same scheme as Adult to attract new customers: casinos and sports betting sites (they pay up to 70% of the money lost by the client who you brought to the site) and shops that sell MP3 tracks, ringtones and pirated software. Also, there is a constant demand for replicas of elite goods. Most often people want pens and lighters (Dupont and Cartier), Swiss watches, bags and wallets (Louis Vuitton, Gucci and Prada). The popularity of online pharmacies can be explained by the fact, that, unlike normal stores, they don't ask for a doctor's prescription to sell anti-depressants, steroids, Viagra and other strong medication. Also, they charge a fraction of what normal stores do. Virtual pharmacies collect orders and send them to India or China where counterfeit medicines are produced. Pharma spammers are responsible for two thirds of the world spam, 40% of which is divided between just two erectile dysfunction products: Viagra and Cialis. The revenue of Glavmed, the largest pharmaceutical company in the world, was estimated to be $120 million before its owner, Igor Gusev, was arrested.

After I took up spamming, I had an idea to combine it with stock exchange speculation. But how?

Baron Daniel Drew, an esteemed 19th century criminal, was a master stock exchange speculator. If he wanted people to sell or buy particular shares, he almost never addressed the matter directly. One of his tricks was walking hastily across the hall of an elite club not far from Wall Street and, taking out his famous red handkerchief, wipe sweat off his forehead. This made him drop a folded piece of paper, as if by accident. Club members jumped at the note, hoping to see a stock exchange prognosis. The contents of the note spread quickly, and soon the members of the club started to sell or buy the shares Drew wanted them to.

Hackers followed a similar strategy when they inserted news about death of Microsoft's founder Bill Gates on CNN homepage. The so-called news quickly got into Chinese mass media, and from there — to the South Korean TV. As a result, the Seoul stock exchange index dropped by 1.5%. According to some estimations, the authors of the hoax made about $5 billion.

You can use mailings to manipulate the stock exchange — all you need to do is share a "secret" of future share growth of small companies. Why small? Because market influence is particularly large for operations with low liquidity. A so-called "pump and dump" strategy can push up prices of such shares by 50% or more.

I acted a little differently. First, I bought cheap shares of little known software companies. Then I used mailings to convince consumers to buy those companies' software. As a result of increased sales, the share price grew and I sold my package. Pump & Dump is an important part of spamming industry and accounts for about 15% of all messages.

Expenses in spam business are incredibly low, so there are hundreds of individual spammers, particularly in Russia. However, there are probably as many as ten highly professional groups of spammers in the world, seven of which originated in Russia.

Even though spam was bringing me a large and steady income, it wasn't making me happy: I had to spend all day in front of the computer, thinking of texts for thousands of advertisement emails, updating domains and website design, keeping the sales statistics. I was annoyed by how monotonous the work was. I realized, with age, that you should only do what you enjoy doing.

CHAPTER 46

SONELAO

"Let's go on vacation," Sonelao, one of my best and oldest clients wrote to me at the beginning of March.

"Why not?" I was excited to get an opportunity to slumber on the beach and flirt with local girls for a couple of weeks. "Where, though? Brazil, Cuba, what about Italy?" I presented my top three.

"Let's go to the Dominican Republic. I don't think you need a visa to go there," Sonelao offered. "But let's stick to it this time, I don't want it to be Thailand all over again."

"Bro, the only reason I couldn't make it to Thailand was because I was shut down two months before the trip. But it was for the best, I guess — we could have got hit by that tsunami. But we were honestly going to come."

"You're right, bro. So, do I book the hotel? Here, look at the pictures."

The hotel in the pictures looked great.

"Just as last time, everything's on me. You don't have to bring any cash at all," Sonelao was making a very generous offer. "Bring your brother along if you want to."

"Alright, friend, we'll think about it."

I had worked with Sonelao since 2004. He was a regular client, one of the most frequent buyers of our dumps. According to him, he was an American of Thai origin, lived in California, drove an expensive BMW and had an army of cash mules that bought stuff in bulk with fake credit cards. He only took American dumps, spending between $5,000 and $10,000 a month. He always paid on time and never asked to wait until he could make a profit off the dumps. Sometimes he sent gifts: perfume, T-shirts, shades and Pirelli calendars. While I was in jail Sonelao kept in touch with my brother over the Internet.

"Dmitry, Sonelao is offering a trip to the Dominican Republic," I messaged my brother. "For a couple of weeks, he's paying. Rum, cigars, smoldering girls…"

"Is it safe?" Dmitry was brief, as always. "He's still our client, and you know what he's buying."

"It is safe for me — I've done my time. Not sure about you, though."

"I think I'm good then. I'd rather go somewhere later, without him. We could take the girls along."

"Suit yourself. I think I'll go."

"Sonelao, book the hotel. I'll be able to go in a couple of weeks," I replied the same evening while opening Google to see if I needed a visa.

Turned out, Belarussians did need a visa to go to the Dominican Republic. The nearest embassy was in Moscow. I went to a store and bought a giant jar of black caviar and a bottle of expensive vodka for Sonelao.

"Bro, I'm flying to Moscow tomorrow to get a visa," I told the American. "You can buy tickets for the middle of March, here's my full name and passport number."

"Sergey, something came up," my friend started, "my passport has expired, I'll have to wait three to four weeks to get a new one."

"I'm afraid that won't do, bro. I really don't want to wait. I've already planned to go on holiday and I will go, with or without you."

"Where to, Dominican Republic?" he asked immediately.

"Haven't decided yet. But I don't think it'll be the Dominican Republic — I don't have that much money at the moment, I've invested in a few projects."

"Money isn't a problem," my friend said. "How much do you need?"

"As you wish. I will send you dumps for the sum later," I answered.

Sonelao transferred me $2,000, and Dmitry, Irina, her friend Anna and I left for Egypt.

CHAPTER 47

YOU HAVE THE RIGHT TO REMAIN SILENT

Ding-ding-ding — I was woken up by someone pressing the doorbell repeatedly. I rubbed my eyes and looked at the clock: it was 6 a.m. Shit, who could it be so early?! Irina? But she's got her own keys. I walked up to the door.

"Who is it?"

"Cleaning," a woman's voice answered.

"What do you want?" I looked into the peephole and indeed saw a lady with a mop.

"Take away the boxes, they're in my way."

"What boxes?" I thought to myself, but for some unclear reason unlocked the front door. Instead of a skinny lady in a cleaning service uniform, I was looking at four sturdy men. The mysterious cleaner was nowhere to be seen. I wonder where they were hiding. Got it — behind the wall on the right — that's the peephole's blind spot. And I was planning to get a new one, with a wider view angle. I tried to close the door, but couldn't: it was caught by a strong hand in a black leather glove. Unfortunately, there wasn't a chain on the door either. It reminded me of all the times I had read (and written) on carding forums something along the lines of, "As far as security is concerned, your flat must be a fortress. If you still haven't installed a second metal door — do it. A chain that won't let the door open too wide, a camera to make sure no one is hiding behind a wall — everything will come in handy. While the police are trying to break into your flat, you'll have plenty of time to format the hard drive or call your lawyer." And there I was, making that very mistake.

"KGB," one of the guests introduced himself. "Here's a search warrant as part of the investigation of the explosions on 3rd July."

Right. On 3rd July, Independence Day a home-made bomb stuffed with metal balls blew up in a crowd in Minsk. There were no casualties, but over fifty people had been wounded. Where was I that day? I was in Gomel, boozing at my friend's country house. Thus, I had an alibi — there were plenty of witnesses.

"May I look at your ID?" I asked the tall officer with short hair, wearing a leather jacket.

"Of course," he took out a small red folder with KGB written over it in gold. According to the ID, I was talking to Colonel Chuchko.

"Go ahead, do your search," I said. I went into the kitchen and, for some reason, poured a glass of champagne and started to sip it.

One of the officers went to get a civil witness. He was away for at least fifteen minutes — it's hard to find someone at 6 a.m. The cops often schedule searches and arrests for the night or early morning when you're yanked out of your warm bed and aren't able to think clearly. Finally, they found one of the neighbors.

"Before we conduct the search you have an opportunity to give up any instruments of crime, large sums of money, weapons, drugs and other illegal objects and substances," said Colonel Chuchko, who appeared to be the leader of the group. "We will register it as 'voluntary submission' — which may come in handy in court."

"Come in handy, right," I thought to myself.

"There is nothing illegal in my house. And I have nothing to do with the explosion, I wasn't even in Minsk when it happened."

CHAPTER 48

THE KGB

I got involved with the KGB by accident. When, in fall 2007, Novik and Miklashevich (the cops who had handled my case) were arrested by the KGB, I testified against them and gave the KGB the voice recording that had been sitting on my desktop. What was I thinking? Why did I get involved with other people's wars? Of course, I wanted to have my way with the men who had sent me behind bars. Human stupidity, indeed, knows no limits.

"Alright, guys," Chuchko interrupted my reminiscences. "Get to work," he ordered his men.

"Would you mind rolling up your sleeves," I intervened, "I don't want anything 'accidentally' falling out of them. You know, something like a bullet or some heroin. And let's not scatter around the flat, search one room after the other. Witnesses, make sure they follow my recommendations, alright?"

Surprisingly, there were no objections.

It goes without saying that they didn't find anything connected to the explosion in my home. To be honest, I had a feeling they weren't even really looking for anything and the whole search was more of a formality they had to go through.

"Now let's have a look at the contents of your computer," a young, fair-haired officer sat down at my laptop and was giving me a questioning look, waiting for the password to log in.

I hesitated — I wasn't sure whether it was a good idea to tell them the password.

"Alright," there wasn't anything interesting for the KGB on my laptop. I sat down at the keyboard and logged in.

My God — I didn't believe my own eyes: I had two crypts open. I had the main encrypted hard drive opened. Shit! What kind of bad luck is this! And it had to happen today of all days. Right, PoliceDog, that's how a quiet life makes you lose your wits. Enjoy the results.

The KGB men were rubbing their hands, looking around the directories, smiling like kids and copying the contents. They were doing what they needed to do and didn't even suspect the surprise awaiting them. I had a nice little program called Deep Freeze installed. It cleaned the system drive after every reboot, and all I had to do now was to use any excuse to restart Windows.

"Hold on," I stopped the fair-headed officer who had already turned off my laptop and was now disconnecting it from the external hard drive, "you can't disconnect it like that, it may crash. You have to start Windows to remove it safely."

"Do it," the officer quickly gave his consent.

"Great, worked like a charm," I thought to myself. "I wish I could see your faces when you show the laptop proudly to your bosses, turn it on and see a blank hard drive."

"Are you done with the laptop?" Colonel Chuchko inquired.

"Yeh, we're taking it with us," the officer replied. "For further investigation," he pronounced slowly.

"Right. Then you two," the colonel pointed at the fair-headed one and another young officer, "are going back to the office, and we're going to search his mother's house."

In half an hour Chuchko, another young officer and I were already in Gatovo — the village where my mother lived, about ten minutes away from the Minsk Ring Road.

"Sergey, we know we're not going to find anything here," Chuchko said, "but we have orders for two searches, so please, go get civil witnesses. Arkady," he looked at his partner, "will write the protocol, you'll sign it and we'll be off."

I invited a neighbor to help, we quickly got the paperwork done and were on our way out of the flat when Chuchko got a phone call. Over the course of the conversation his face changed several times until his expression was one of utter discontent and unpleasant surprise.

"What are the passwords for encrypted containers?" he barked at me.

"I don't remember." When I realized Deep Freeze had worked, I started to speak differently. "I changed it yesterday when I was drunk, wrote down the new password, and I can't recall where."

"Alright. We'll lock you up for ten days and see if it helps your memory."

I tried to remember the information I had on my encrypted hard drives: ICQ without chat logs, VISA Interchange Directory — a database used for determining the type of the card and the bank from the BIN, hundreds of millions of emails for porn lovers, sales statistics, a file with a list of people that owed me money, contacts, a couple of porn videos with Angel Dark — my favorite actress. In short, nothing of particular interest for the KGB.

Should I say it? To hell with it, as long as it gets them off my back.

"Alright, I'll write them down," I told Chuchko the passwords.

He dialed a number — I guess of the person that had called him a few minutes earlier, and read out my passwords. It seemed to have satisfied his counterpart, because then we left the flat, got into the car and went to the KGB's offices.

"Well, Sergey," Arkady addressed me when I was sitting in his office, "let's negotiate your involvement as a witness on the explosion case? It's just a formality. You don't know anything about it, do you?"

"You got it right — I don't. Where's my laptop?"

"What do you mean where? Next door…"

"What do you mean next door?" I didn't like the what suddenly began to dawn on me.

"At the Cyber Crime Department."

"The Cyber Crime Department?!" the answer caught me completely off-guard.

"Well," Arkady, a KGB investigator, shrugged in dismay, "it's simple. There were four of us, right?"

I nodded.

"Chuchko and I are from the KGB, and the other two are from the police. Your laptop's no use to us, but those guys know their stuff with electronics."

Crap! I got fooled like a first-grader. Why didn't I check everyone's

ID? Now I understood why they didn't even try to look for anything: the cops just needed my computer and the men from the KGB didn't care at all — they knew I had nothing to do with the bomb.

"You really fell foul of the cops," the investigator continued, "the operation against you was coordinated by Naumov, the Head of National Police."

Fell foul of the police. I bet I have: I testified against two of their employees, offered evidence and helped to reveal a few rogue cops. They must have found out the information was coming from me. You got it in the neck, PoliceDog. Trusted the KGB to turn a blind eye to criminal traces that are always on your computer...

"You can only lie to the woman you love and a police officer..." Arkady seemed to have read my thoughts.

"What are you on about?"

"You should tell the truth to everyone else," he finished. "I was talking about your passwords."

"You're right there, that was stupid on my part."

"Don't blame yourself," he looked at me with a look that seemed to be both sympathy and compassion, "if you hadn't told us the passwords, we would have given you thiopental sodium ("the truth serum") — you would have told us much more."

"Nice methods you got here, guys," I summarized gloomily.

"Alright, sign the protocol and let's go."

"Where?!" I looked at him in alarm, then looked out of the window into the KGB's backyard.

"The cops want to speak with you."

CHAPTER 49

FAMILIAR TERRITORY

The National Police headquarters was a short walk from the yellow monster with white columns that was the KGB building.

"Name?" we were seen in by an unfriendly officer.

"Pavlovich…"

Arkady left.

"Take off the chain, the pendant, sunglasses and empty your pockets and put your money and mobile phones on the table," the major ordered, while I was losing hope to ever get out of this place with every word. "Don't forget the belt and shoe laces."

That's it. Welcome back. Well, Sergey, you should have thought about this earlier. Preferably, before telling them your passwords.

"Will you give my things to my mother?" I asked.

"Everything except the phones. Write a declaration in the investigator's name."

"And who would the investigator be?" I inquired.

"Belsky."

I took the pen and wrote a declaration. In duplicate. And when, twenty minutes later, Belsky appeared (and turned out to be a medium-height thickset high-browed investigator aged about thirty), I gave him both copies and asked him to sign the list of my belongings.

"Why's that?" he seemed surprised.

"Just in case. Last time your people took about $2,000 worth of stuff from my car, even a half-empty bottle of perfume. I wrote down my mother's phone number, call her and tell her to send my lawyer, Yelena Shevchenko.

"Alright," he agreed.

The lawyer arrived in an hour. With all the powers of my imagination I couldn't believe the short, plumpish middle-aged woman was the attractive 35-year-old Yelena Shevchenko I knew.

"Umm, where's Yelena?" I asked the woman.

"She doesn't work as a lawyer anymore, she's a judge now. She recommended me to your mother — Yelena and I used to work together. Though, you know how it is with lawyers in our country."

"You guys can't do much?" I suggested.

"No, we can't. Not in our courts," the lawyer concluded.

And that's how a new character appeared in the story of my life, the lawyer Marina Mikhailovna — a simple woman who smoked a lot and didn't have any illusions about legitimacy in our country.

"I understand what's going on," she said. "I'll see you again when you're in Volodarka."

She said goodbye and left, tearing another connection I had with the outside world. The cops put me into a car and we went back to my flat for a second search.

"We are going to draw up a search warrant," said one of the officers, "and you can use the time to collect the things you'll need at the pre-trial detention center."

Right, the pre-trial detention center. It feels horrible to collect your own things to go to jail. It's one thing when you're arrested in the street: they press your face into the pavement and tell you not to move. It's a completely different thing to be in your own flat with three cops and understand the arrest is inevitable, and you have to get your own things to take with you to jail. At least the cops were decent and allowed me enough time to get ready.

A sports suit, a knitted hat, warm gloves, a down jacket (alternatively: a long sheepskin or quilted jacket) will come in handy on the floor in cold cells of jail, several pairs of warm socks, thermals, a cheap pair of shoes (people at the pre-trial detention center don't care how expensive your shoes are — they will take out arch support anyways), a towel, soap, toilet paper, a toothbrush and toothpaste, pens, notebooks, envelopes, a watch, tea, coffee, sweets, chocolate, sugar, stock cubes, a bottle of water, a couple of blocks of cigarettes, matches, a plastic cup, plate, spoon, water boiler, medicine (painkillers and something for a blocked nose and upset stomach), a photo of the woman you love. You write a note that says, "I love you. Whatever happens". And off you go. For all you know, you will be away for years.

Do you want to know what happened next? The usual: a visit to the prosecutor, whom I didn't manage to talk to in person this time, an arrest warrant, the grey walls of pre-trial detention facility with the furrowed concrete walls that are supposed to pressure your delicate psyche and are banned in the civilized world, dim light, rats and hordes of bedbugs that turn your body into a giant buffet. I wish I could turn into a mosquito and fly away from here... I'd go and visit grandad.

CHAPTER 50

WHO IS MR. GONZALEZ?

Albert "Segvec" Gonzalez at the annual computer hacker convention DefCon, 2001

When I stepped into the investigator's office, my lawyer chose an odd way to greet me,

"Who is Albert Gonzalez?"

"I'd rather you told me what date it is," I shot back.

"The 8th August 2008," the lawyer muttered perplexedly, not understanding why I asked.

"So… I've been here for eight days already. Good day, Marina!"

"Wow, you remember my name. Great job!" she complemented me. "Why are you here, in Zhodino, and not in Minsk?"

I had been moved from the pre-trial detention center in Minks — Volodarka — to a prison in Zhodino, about 50 miles from the Belarusian capital.

"My cellmate in Volodarka said that it was because the guards had figured out I was 'too comfortable' by reading my letters," I told my lawyer.

"So who is Mr. Gonzalez?"

"What Gonzalez?!"

"Your associate."

"My who?" I gave my lawyer a baffled look.

"Your associate, your pal, your buddy — call him as you like, it's doesn't matter."

"I don't remember any associates of that name."

"Here, look what the journalists are writing about you," Marina took a pile of newspapers out of her briefcase and handed them to me.

I skimmed the articles, which detailed a huge cyber-crime conspiracy.

CHAPTER 51

GONZALEZ, SUVOROV, YASTREMSKIY

Maksim Yastremskiy, a.k.a. Maksik

Albert Gonzalez was born in Miami to a family of Cuban immigrants. He got his first computer at the age of eight when the Internet was only just starting to develop. At nine, Albert knew how to protect his computer from viruses. He didn't go out or play football with his friends — instead he spent his days at the computer. After a while, their son's hobby started to worry his parents: his mother would put him to bed and then catch him at the computer at two in the morning. When Gonzalez was seventeen, he and two of his classmates used their school computers to hack the Indian government's official website. Gonzalez wasn't allowed anywhere near a computer for six months for that stunt. In 1999, he finished school and moved to New York. Under the nickname SoupNazi, which he borrowed from Seinfeld, he used Internet chatrooms to meet people who would become his associates. Four years later, he started breaking into U.S. computer networks.

Gonzalez was arrested in 2003 by the US Secret Service but he didn't want to go to jail and agreed to assist the federals in Operation Firewall, aimed at carding and hacking website ShadowCrew.com, also known as "the cybercrime supermarket".

Moving on. Alexander Suvorov. He grew up in Sillamae, a small town in northeast Estonia. Sillamae is quite a special place: it was a closed town during the Soviet period because it housed a secret defense industry plant. Unsurprisingly, most of the people who lived there were highly qualified engineers and technicians. Right after graduating in 2002, Suvorov left Sillamae and only returned a couple of times. He barely kept in touch with his former classmates.

That year — 2002 — Gonzalez was among eleven people (including three Ukrainians and one Belorussian) charged in the U.S. with a criminal conspiracy; hacking into computer networks, fraud and selling stolen credit and debit card numbers. At the time, it was the largest case of its type in the USA.

The gang chose victims from Fortune Magazine's list of the world's

500 largest corporations, checked their payment and security systems, and then broke into their networks. Gonzalez also toured US cities with his laptop, using a special program to get into shops' computer networks. Gonzalez used Wi-Fi to look for vulnerable networks. If it worked out, he used his computer to copy credit card data (card numbers, PIN-codes and account information) onto servers located in the USA, the Netherlands, Latvia and Ukraine. Later, investigators would find over 41 million credit card numbers on just two of the servers. In total, the hackers stole the data of 200 million debit and credit cards. Some of the stolen cards were sold on the black market and some were used by the criminals themselves: they recorded data onto blank plastic cards to cash out tens of thousands of dollars at ATMs.

The Americans also found out who the closest colleagues of Gonzalez were: Suvorov and Maksim Yastremskiy (a.k.a. Maksik) from Ukraine. Suvorov's online nickname was JonnyHell — the very same guy with whom I had worked closely together and who I had gone to visit in Moscow.

After a tip-off by the Americans, Yastremskiy was arrested in July 2007 while on holiday in Turkey. On 3rd March 2008, the 24-year-old Suvorov was arrested in Frankfurt on his way to Bali, apparently by FBI special agents.

"Including three Ukrainians and a Belarussian…" my lawyer repeated. "Looks like Gonzalez was your associate. Or the other way around," she added.

"Looks like it. I thought I was selling JonnyHell's dumps. Turns out, they belonged to Gonzalez," I sighed. "I didn't know Yastremskiy personally, but I once bought a fake Ukrainian passport from him.

And I must say, the quality was terrible. So, I guess Yastremskiy began his criminal career with forging documents."

"Suvorov, Yastremskiy and Gonzalez described their life motto as 'Get rich or die trying'"

"They didn't come up with it. I think it was Fifty Cent, a rapper."

"Do you get letters here?"

"Yes, I got one from my mum yesterday. Have you seen the investigator?"

"We spoke on the phone. He said he wasn't planning to see you any time soon. He advised us to follow news about your case in the news. By the way, here, have a look at the official press-release on your case," Marina held out a few sheets of paper, held together with a safety pin. "It was on the U.S. Department of Justice's website," she added proudly.

"Alright, I have to go," Marina rose from her chair and started to collect her papers. "I will try to help you. I mean, I will do all I can — yours is not the most ordinary of cases. Also, it's being coordinated by the Prosecutor General himself. Your mum has brought some food for you, she's waiting in the car with Irina."

"Good. Tell them I said hi," I said goodbye and left.

I returned to the cell after walking 400 meters along a complicated network of underground corridors, divided by a few dozens of metal doors, lay down on the bed and closed my eyes.

CHAPTER 52

RIGHTS THAT MAKE YOU RIGHT

The days that follow merged into lingering and insufferable inactivity where the days looked so much alike they felt as if they'd been photocopied. When it happened for the first time, I knew what I was in jail for: I was on the most-wanted list of four law enforcement agencies all over the world and was under arrest for something I'd done. This time, however, everything looked more like a nightmare that wouldn't go away no matter how hard I pinched myself.

"You know, I'm beginning to realize I've never loved anyone like I loved you," Irina wrote to me in one of her letters. "It feels so nice to understand you live through one person. It's so hard to find "the one", and I got lucky... what is happening now is just justice having a vacation in August."

Judging by the state of events, justice took a long vacation. In September, I was still in the pre-trial detention center and nothing seemed to be changing.

When you get sent behind the bars, you find yourself deprived of many things you're used to: your cell phone, your watch, comfortable clothes and so on. And it makes you feel at a loss. A couple of weeks ago mum sent me my favorite watch, a comfortable pair of jeans, my sweater, Irina's photo and a scarf — the scarf that Irina knitted for me last New Year. It smelt of her perfume. Small things, you say? But in jail you miss vivid impressions, and you don't care about the things you are sent as much as about the very fact you're not being abandoned. News from family, any token of attention, can elevate your mood for quite a while.

These gloomy walls destroy one's ability to feel, touch and see. You become a robot: you eat when you have to, you smoke to take your mind off things, and you wait. You wait here all the time: you wait for walks, care packages, the investigator, the lawyer, letters. Irina didn't write that often. The snoring of my cellmates grew more annoying day by day.

Chairs are made of steel. Beds are made of steel. Doors are made of steel. Everything is made of steel, except my nerves.

Last night before I fell asleep I caught myself thinking about suicide for the first time. I was lying in the dark with tears in my eyes. I was imagining what I'd write in my last letter. Such ideas got me scared of my own thoughts.

I really wanted to share my worries with someone, but there wasn't anyone. It's foolish to even imagine discussing anything like this with your cellmates. Also, confining in someone would be a purely egotistical step.

CHAPTER 53

THERE'S A BLACK SHEEP IN EVERY FLOCK

The investigator finally arrived. He turned out to be a stout man in his early thirties wearing an expensive, but tacky, striped suit.

"My name is Alexander Sushko," he introduced himself.

"I've been waiting for you for ages," there was no need for me to introduce myself in return — I was pretty sure most of his police department not only knew me, but also hated me passionately.

"Do you want to know how we picked up your trail?"

"I know already. You made a little deal with the KGB to search my flat, got access to my laptop and now I've got a nice new criminal case."

"You shouldn't have given them the passwords." Sushko lifted his hands in mock dismay. "There wouldn't have been a case if you had kept them to yourself — there isn't a technology to decipher passwords that long."

"The KGB are sellout bastards. They knew I was helping their investigation against rogue cops from your department, and still handed me over."

"Well, they got the information they needed from you and managed to get you arrested. Two birds with one stone. Do you see what kind of people they are now?"

"A bunch of backstabbers…"

"So it appears. But I actually wasn't talking about that or you personally. I meant how we picked up trail of your gang."

"What gang? I don't see anyone else being arrested."

"That's not what the Americans think. Have you seen the press-release?" The effort Sushko had to put into pronouncing 'press release,' a foreign word, betrayed him as a person somewhat ashamed of his lower-middle class roots.

"Yes, I have. Marina showed it to me," I exchanged looks with my lawyer.

"Look at this document then," the investigator reached into his briefcase and held out an indictment entitled "The United States of America vs. Albert Gonzalez."

"According to our information, you were part of this organization," he added. "Here, look," Sushko fished out a document with a "U.S. District Court" stamp from his massive folder. "Did you know the U.S. Secret Service paid Gonzalez $75,000 a year?"

"What for?" Sushko's words made me nervous.

"Did you hear about Operation Firewall?"

"Nothing aside the fact dozens of America's most notorious carders got arrested," I tried to remember something else.

"Listen to this story: in May 2004, Gonzalez, one of the ShadowCrew forum's administrators, made an offer that got a lot of attention. He offered users access to a private, ShadowCrew-only, VPN-service.

Do you know what VPN is?"

"Of course. A Virtual Private Network is typically used to grant remote access to a corporate network from an employee's home. But this isn't why it attracts carders. VPN also encrypts every bit of information that passes through it, which makes it secure."

"Right. But VPN-servers have a disadvantage not a lot of people know about: everything that goes through the network can be tracked from a central hub. Gonzalez reassured everyone it was safe. But what the forum dwellers didn't know was that nine months earlier the U.S. police had arrested Gonzalez while he was trying to cash out a stolen credit card. He was questioned, and the Secret Service soon knew the truth: the 21-year-old son of Cuban immigrants was renting an apartment for $700 a month, had a $12,000 credit card debt and was officially unemployed. That's how they convinced him to become an informer. The VPN-service was a particularly successful trick. The equipment was bought with police money and they received an official permit to record all activity. That's how a "carders-only" VPN-service became the perfect bait. ShadowCrew's best carders fell into the trap — and paid $30 to $50 a month to do so. Gonzalez received $75,000 a year from the U.S. government for his work. Between April 2003 and October 2004, FBI agents were monitoring all ShadowCrew's activity and building up their evidence base. The operation was once almost sabotaged: Ethics, one of ShadowCrew's hackers, broke into T-Mobile and stole documents from one of the FBI agent's laptops. He then uploaded them to the forum as evidence that the forum was being monitored. However, Gonzalez, who was the head of the forum at the time, managed to persuade users to ignore it. On 26th October 2004, the 21 most active members of the carding community were arrested all around the world, ShadowCrew ceased to exist, and informant Gonzalez returned to his Miami home. Well played, eh?"

"There is a black sheep in every flock. How did you find out Yastremskiy was connected to Gonzalez? As far as I know he worked with JonnyHell."

"The FBI analyzed Yastremskiy's account with the E-gold payment system and found he transferred $410,750 to an account of a certain 'Segvec' between February and May 2006. They pulled on that string and discovered Gonzalez, also known as Segvec, was supplying Yastremskiy with dumps."

CHAPTER 54

PRISON NO. 8

"Can you bring me more pens?" I asked Marina at the beginning of January.

"I brought you two last time. Have you used them up?" the lawyer opened her bag and gave me a few more pens.

"They were taken away."

"By who?"

"We are searched after we leave the office to make sure we don't take anything illegal into the cell."

"Since when are ball-pens illegal?"

"A guard, an 18-year-old jerk, asked me where I got them."

"What did you say?"

"I said my lawyer gave them to me so I'll have something to write with. He said they were illegal and I had to throw them away. So, I did. But I broke them first, so the asshole didn't get them."

"Sergey, lying is a sin in the eyes of God, but a convenient thing in the face of the circumstances! You could have said you took them with you from the cell."

"I could have."

"Do you know what you need?"

"What?"

"You need to learn to lie. In a world where everybody lies, the truth mostly brings trouble."

Once Prison No. 8 in Zhodino, where I was being held, was known for being the strictest prison in Belarus. But today, this title has passed to the pre-trial detention center in Vitebsk. The reason? The former head of Prison No. 8, was transferred there. But his ghost is still haunting the underground galleries of No. 8. Prison employees still believe their former boss to be a semi-god.

They start putting pressure on you here as soon as you get out of the police car. When a guard enters a cell, everyone must stand up and say "Good day, officer." Then the inmate on duty says his full name, date of birth and his crime — only then will the cops start to ask why the aluminum mugs are dirty (prisoners are given sand to polish their mugs). If the mugs are clean, they will inspect the water closet tap. It is common knowledge prison guards can find a problem anywhere.

Human rights here are violated on a daily basis. You can't receive books from home, which violates the right of self-education. And even though you get access to the prison library every two or three weeks, you can't possibly call that outdated Communist propaganda literature. Prisoners aren't allowed to wear shorts or sleeveless tops, even when the temperature rises above 40 centigrade. They make you shave regularly despite only one disposable razor being allowed per five people and some of your cellmates may have Hepatitis or even HIV. Same thing with scissors — you only get one pair, usually in terrible condition, for use by the whole floor. That's why we normally used razor blades for clipping (or, rather, cutting off) our fingernails. Sometimes we simply bit them off. Bed linen is washed weekly, but for some reason only one sheet at a time.

The food is terrible: portions are tiny and the main dish is fish soup, sprat spread and pickled cabbage in all possible variations. They give us more or less decent food on Tuesdays, when the prison administration does their weekly check-up. Porridge in the morning and pea soup and pasta for lunch. Once they didn't give (or even sell) us salt for four months. We had to cut food with thread or illegal knives we made from disposable razor blades, risking going to the isolation cell for fifteen days.

The prison store sells toothpaste in tin tubes and suggests squeezing it out into a plastic bag because inmates aren't allowed to have anything in a metal container. They would put shaving foam into a plastic bag as well. If you buy cigarettes at the store, you'll have to give them empty packs, which get carefully counted. And, until very recently, every single cigarette in Belarusian prisons was snapped in half. To this day no-one is sure what the cops were hoping to find inside.

Despite the cells being overcrowded, running water and electricity are shut off at 10 p.m. (bed time). When you get assigned to a cell, you don't get your mattress and blanket until the following morning, so you'll have to sleep on the floor or the table. We aren't allowed to sleep during the day either. I once asked a guard:

"Why don't you let us sleep during the day? Everyone knows, the more you sleep the less you break the law."

"Here we think an inmate must get tired enough during the day not to think about escaping at night," he answered.

There is a bath house (which is in fact a simple shower) on every floor, but you have to walk there wearing only your underwear.

Walks are obligatory and you can't opt out. You will go for a walk even if it means standing in the pouring rain for two hours.

Letters from No. 8 take up to 12 days to reach their destination. And if you don't have an envelope, you won't be able to file a single official complaint. You can't complain about the personnel either — not a single word you write will make it outside of the building.

Prisoners here are afraid of inspections and for good reasons: special attention will be paid to the cell, which means all extra dishes, mugs and so on will be confiscated. It doesn't help to ask any questions — cops have an answer to everything. Even the smallest and the most insignificant officer enjoys being called Mr. and demands everyone do it.

We have to do a general clean before the inspection. We roll up the mattresses, put them on the bed, splash four buckets of water on the floor and wash it until all the soapy foam is gone.

Guards punish the smallest act of disobedience or misconduct by taking away all the board games from the cell and constantly threaten us they will shut off the only electric socket. I guess this is why there aren't any TVs — not to give the cops another pressure lever.

There are rumors of so-called "pressure cells" — cells where you are beaten as soon as you cross the doorway and until you sign a guilty plea. Guards typically support such rumors to spread fear among newcomers.

Of course, the prisoners are also at fault in the fact the guards are able to create and maintain such regime. One must understand that, unlike Volodarka, which is located in the capital, No. 8 has always been more remote and most inmates come from neighboring villages and small towns. They are uneducated and browbeaten, many of who haven't seen much of life beside beatings and the nearest liquor store. So, when a prison guard offers them the choice of filing a report on a convict or simply hitting him twice, they choose the later.

The staff of Prison No. 8 don't just do their job — they hate us. They scream at us, beat us (even though we are legally innocent until proven guilty), which creates constant discomfort, fear and pressure. Of course, you get used to anything, but your body is still living under constant stress and you can't wait to be transferred to a different jail.

CHAPTER 55

TALL TALES

"I am no God Almighty," investigator Sushko started one conversation at the beginning of February, "but I can make sure you get a minimum sentence — six years. You will have to hand over your protectors from the KGB."

"Thank you, but don't bother. You can keep these tall tales for someone else."

"You don't have to decide now. Think about it, Sergey, really think about it."

"I will testify in court — you won't get anything from me."

"As you wish," I couldn't tell from the investigator's face if he was disappointed by my rejection, or simply did not care. "Here are photocopies of a few documents for you to sign."

I looked at the first document. It was a complete log of my Internet connections showing the date and time of my Internet sessions and the IP-addresses I used, provided by my Internet operator.

It turned out the police had used a traffic sniffer on my Internet provider to spy on my online activities the whole time I'd been living in that flat. Every log was then analyzed with a program called NetResident.

"How could I have protected myself from that?" I knew the answer already, but I wanted to hear it from Sushko.

"Only by getting online using a 3G modem registered in someone else's name, of course, or via Wi-Fi — I'm sure there are plenty of badly-protected Wi-Fi networks in your area. Also, it goes without saying you should never tell anyone which Internet provider you're using." I could dislike my opponent as much as I wanted, but his reply was brilliant.

The second document was a list of transactions made by my brother's bank card.

I was surprised by how much you can learn from a simple bank transaction list. From my brother's regular use, his favorite bar is Pristan (on average three visits per week), his favorite restaurant is Miami Blues, his favorite perfume store is Brokar and favorite grocery store is Furshet. It is obvious he smokes (he frequents a cigar shop) and drives a car with a powerful engine (on 5th December he spent $51 on gas — given an approximate gas price of $0.8 per liter that's about 70 liters) and has a female partner (a $366 purchase at a lingerie shop).

All purchases except the last two were made in Ukraine. On 21st March 2008, he went shopping in Duty Free at Kyiv's Borispol airport and the next transaction was made in Egypt. We Google "jollie ville" and find out he was staying at Jollie Ville hotel in Sharm el Sheikh. Voila!

"Add hundreds of surveillance cameras in every modern city," the way I was obviously captivated by the document didn't escape Sushko's vigilant eye.

"Why don't you want to let me go on bail?" I changed the topic to something I was more interested in.

"Who says we don't?!" the investigator's face displayed fake surprise. "We have discussed it at the department. A million U.S. dollars and you're free to go."

"Have you lost your goddamn mind? What million?"

CHAPTER 56

HUNGER STRIKE

In March, my third application for bail was turned down. Shortly before that, my investigator had prolonged my detention again, despite promising me otherwise. I objected to the extension in court, filed a complaint to Prosecutor General's office and started a hunger strike.

A hunger strike — a voluntary rejection of food in Prison No. 8 happens as follows. First, you're taken to a small holding cell (1.5 meter by x 2.5 meters) where the temperature doesn't rise above 10 centigrade — you'll have to sleep in three pairs of trousers, two sweaters, a down jacket, a hat and gloves and you'll still be cold. The bed is only available at night, and even then it doesn't have a mattress. The window won't open, you don't get to go on walks or smoke. You're allowed to take only a few personal belongings (I hardly managed to sneak in a bar of soap, a toothbrush and a towel), write (pens and paper are confiscated) or read — they won't give you any newspapers or letters. They won't give you any hot water. Some prisoners aren't even allowed to take warm clothes. And it'll be impossible to reach any sort of authority figure in the prison.

I don't know how soon the prison administration is supposed to inform the prosecutor and investigator of your hunger strike, but over here they don't do it at all. The administration makes sure the conditions you're put in will break you.

You feel the hungriest between the 16th and 18th hour after you stop eating. After that, you pretty much forget the feeling of hunger.

Four days later my lawyer appeared.

"You can wrap up your strike," she said. "The prosecution has responded, they say it was the last time they will extend your detention, you'll get to see your case soon."

"Thank God — finally things got a little clearer."

"Why did you even start this? In Belarus, a hunger strike is a completely ineffective form of protest, no-one pays it any attention. Also, rejecting food is a serious violation of prison rules. The pre-trial detention center administration really doesn't like it and you can even end up in a punishment cell — the ones with wet concrete floors and bare walls. How do you like that idea?"

"I mentioned it in my complaint, so I had to follow through."

"Alright, you got what you wanted. Now we've got to wait for the investigator to compile the case."

The very same day I was taken back to my old cell.

CHAPTER 57

HELPING OUR ENEMIES

"Have you heard they arrested police Colonel Miklashevich?" Marina asked me the day after I finished my hunger strike.

"God's not a sucker!" Miklashevich was the one involved in my arrest, who later tried to recruit me.

"What do you mean?"

"The whole department decided what my bail should be. They agreed on a million," I explained. "They thought it was funny. Now two of them are behind bars."

"It doesn't make our lives any easier, though. Sushko is going to be here soon, he left shortly after I did. By the way, a deputy chief now — Makarevich had to quit, things weren't looking too bright for him. And Sushko has taken his place."

The first document Sushko showed me that day was an indictment signed by a U.S. Secret Service agent.

Sonelao had been one of my best clients, a.k.a. Surfrider, a.k.a. Mr. Towellie, a.k.a. Richard Druc, owner of Surfrider Boards, a.k.a.… Ryan Knisley, a USSS special agent.

"Do you see now why he wouldn't go to the Dominican Republic with you?" Sushko asked.

"It's crystal clear. He was waiting for a court to give him permission to arrest me. Right in the airport. And I can imagine what sort of prison my brother and I would have ended up in if our Thailand trip had actually happened in 2004."

"Do you remember that story about Ivanov and Gorshkov, the Russian hackers invited to work in the USA who got arrested on arrival?"

"It rings a bell. I think it was back in 2000, two kids, aged 20 and 19. From the Ural Mountains," I tried to remember something that happened ten years ago.

"They were from Chelyabinsk. They were blackmailing American companies. First, they scanned the victim's network for vulnerabilities. When they found them, the hackers got in touch with the company's system administrator, usually via email. They usually said they were a group of computer experts who specialized in testing protection for software servers and payment systems. They said they were outside of the US, in a country where it wasn't illegal. This was followed with a list of the vulnerabilities they had discovered. The administrator was then advised to tell his boss to pay for them not to destroy the server next time. They requested about $200 from small companies, and tens of thousands of dollars from larger ones.

They mostly targeted online casinos (which stored credit card information), bank servers and Internet service providers. Among the companies affected were Online Information Bureau (lost tens of thousands credit cards), Speaksay.net Internet provider, Korean Bank in Los Angeles and even Western Union. When CD Universe music store refused to pay the hackers the requested $100,000, thousands of their customers' credit cards appeared on public websites. Ivanov and Gorshkov were so sure of their invulnerability that they would often leave text files containing something like "Alex was here" on hacked servers. What's more, the hackers offered their services as security consultants. Ivanov would send out his CV, which even had his photograph.

The Americans sent information about Ivanov's business to the Russian police, but were simply ignored. It was obvious the hacker wouldn't be arrested in Russia. He had to be lured to the USA. So, FBI agents created Invita Technologies, a non-existent computer company, and offered Ivanov a job as their security expert. Of course, first he would have to have an interview in Seattle. The FBI were more than happy to pay for his plane tickets. Ivanov didn't just buy it, he also dragged Gorshkov along as his business partner.

During the interview, the FBI agents posing as Invita Technologies staff persuaded Ivanov to hack into a few sites and chatted to Gorshkov about obtaining credit card information

At the same time, a computer expert from Washington University that the FBI had invited to play the role of another Invita's executive, got into the computer Ivanov was using to break into websites for the interview, opened a pre-installed key-logger (a program that "remembers" the sequence of typed keys) to get the password that Ivanov used to remotely access his computer back in Chelyabinsk, which had the programs he had used for cyber-attacks.

Vasily Gorshkov was sentenced to three years of prison and a $690,000 fine, and his associate, Alexey Ivanov, got four years."

"Looks like Sonelao's plans to take me to Thailand, and then to Dominicana failed."

"Looks like it. The FBI managed to lure Yastremskiy to Turkey," Marina joined in. "And despite the fact everything on his laptop was encrypted, a few days in a Turkish prison made him tell them his seventeen-digit password."

"Two punches in the kidneys will get you any password," I tried to joke. "I'd rather know this, though: an international warrant for my arrest was signed on 28th April. Since then I've been to Ukraine, Dubai and the Maldives. How is that possible?"

"That's not that uncommon, Interpol can't spread information that quickly," Sushko told me.

I stared glumly at him.

"For some reason, you people keep thinking you're the smartest," he continued. "A lot of guys now behind bars keep asking themselves, 'Where did I make a mistake? How did they get me?' We cops understand the rule of the game better each day. I don't think it'll come as a secret to you that there are undercover cops in most organized crime groups, spies in secret production plants and informants following world's greatest politicians. It would be weird if the American law enforcement didn't have the brains to get their people into the carding community.

"You sometimes make it seem like in the States every other carder is a rat."

"Well, what are you going to do? The strategy of using informants has been successfully used to fight organized crime since the 1980s."

"But things are different here. People don't sell each other out so much, I guess."

"Have you seen the American Criminal Code? At least half of all crimes carries a life sentence. Criminals try to ease their own burden — about 87% of defendants plead guilty and hand over everyone and everything just to get a shorter sentence."

"Who asked you to send your partner-in-crime your own photo, tell them your brother's bank account details, your mum's home address for shipping goods and share personal details?" Marina asked me with incredulity after the investigator left.

"We often give our enemies the very weapons they need to destroy us," I remembered Aesop.

CHAPTER 58

ROGUE COPS

At the beginning of the summer, I was transferred to Volodarka. It had the same atmosphere, the same problems and even a lot of the same people as three years before. As if I had never got out. Déjà vu...

In the holding cell, I bumped into Vladimir Boyankov, my old associate, who was now under arrest as part of the same case as the crooked cops who had offered their service to me: Novik and Miklashevich.

"Hey there, Vladimir!" I was happy to see his unshaven face. "Go on, tell me how you managed to get in trouble with the cops."

"What, you haven't seen the newspapers?"

"On the contrary, I have. Apparently, at the beginning of 2006 police Colonel Sergey Novik created a criminal group to use self-made counterfeit credit cards to steal money from ATMs. According to the investigation's estimations, over the course of its existence (from February 2006 to October 2007) the group stole about $340,000. Miklashevich had help of cyber-criminals with how to manufacture fake cards and record data onto magnetic stripes of blank cards. According to the General Prosecutor's Office, Novik, as chief organizer of the criminal activities, made sure all members of the group were supplied with working counterfeit cards, PIN-codes and information about card-accounts of the actual owners. Having divided the roles up, he was supposedly responsible for protection, which he provided using his day job: prosecutor flagged Novik's connections to the employees of bank processing centers that were checking transactions carried out with fake credit cards. Am I right?"

"Well, yes. In general. Novik worked out a relatively safe system that allowed us to avoid arrest for a long time."

"What scheme?"

"The first rule was 'Don't steal where you live.' We only cashed cards outside of Belarus (in Russia). Second, we were constantly on the go: "One day — one city". You cash out as much as possible half an hour before midnight, then the card's daily limit is renewed, and you cash out as much as possible after midnight. Then the card is thrown away — despite potentially being good to use for many days to come. That's the third rule."

How did the story end? Boyankov grew lazy and started to work in Belarus. One of the ATMs "swallowed" a few cards, and managed to photograph Boyankov's face, which, it goes without saying, had been on a wanted list for ages. Cops from a town called Zaslavl, where it happened, recognized Boyankov from the mugshot and launched a criminal case. Colonel Novik phoned Zaslavl and made sure the case was transferred to Minsk, where it was successfully lost. Then Novik and the rest told Boyankov what's what and forbade him from working in Belarus ever again. He disobeyed and got caught again. This time the case was started in Minsk. It was suggested to Boyankov he take a couple of years vacation behind bars. But he didn't want to go alone, so he wrote a letter to the Prosecutor General, explaining every detail of his association with Novik and Miklashevich…

CHAPTER 59

THINGS ARE MOVING, GENTLEMEN OF THE JURY!

Me in the court room, August, 2009

The hearing began on 6th August — a year after I was arrested. Judge Yermolenkov, a lean man of boyish demeanor only a couple of years older than me, announced twenty minutes after the start that my guilt had been completely proven, and there was no need to ask me any questions.

On 13th August, at the end of the fifth hearing, the prosecuting lawyer finally woke up. He hadn't said a single word or asked a single question throughout the hearing, he wasn't even sure how to use email.

"Why do you need eight email adresses???" the judge asked me at one point, puzzled. "One is quite enough for me and the prosecutor." "I don't even have an email," the trial attorney admitted, responsibly. (None of this, however, stopped him from considering my charges to be comprehensively proven and asking for a prison sentence of fourteen and a half years for selling American dumps to an American special agent.)

I must say Belarusian justice is, in general, harsh. Judges throw around prison sentences so long it would be physically impossible to serve them. During Soviet times, 5 years were considered serious, but now you can get 25 and even 30 years! Judges must believe convicts live as long as patriarchs from the Old Testament — but an average Belarussian man dies at 65.

It's good mum wasn't there to witness the show. Only Irina and Nikolay, one of my best friends, were in the court room. They sit looking down at their shoes as if they don't even know me. Irina is clutching her purse and fighting back tears. And Nikolay seems to be feeling guilty he can't help me. "Look at me, look at me," I kept asking them silently. "I'm still here, still with you. I know it's hard. It's unbearable to take part in this farce, but don't pretend I don't exist anymore…"

On the morning of 24th August, the day of the sentence, the judge made an offer via my lawyer,

"Yermolenkov is strongly suggesting you plead guilty," she told me.

"And what will I get in return?"

"You'll get two years less."

"Less than what?"

"I asked him the same question. He said, less than the number he had in mind."

"Marina, he might have fifteen years or something in mind. Tell him to go to hell with that offer."

"Alright."

The same day I was found guilty on all five articles listed in the indictment and given a ten-year sentence. With confiscation of property. The most amazing part though, was that the judge made a mistake and gave me a sentence that contradicted what is legally stipulated — he was supposed to give me twelve years at the very least.

That evening I wrote to Irina that, in light of such a sentence, continuing our relationship has no point.

CHAPTER 60

PRISON IS THE EASY PART

Transporting prisoners from the railway carriage to the penal colony

I was still in the pre-trial detention center a month after the sentence, and only in the beginning of October was I transferred. An invisible prison guard came up to our cell and, without opening the peep hole, said, "Pavlovich, out, with personal belongings."

For some reason, the things you really wait for happen unexpectedly. When I was finally told to leave, my bags weren't packed (you have to list every item separately) and some of my clothes were being washed.

The railway carriages used for transporting prisoners are known as Stolypinsky wagons or simply a Stolypin. During the time of Russian Prime Minister Pyotr Stolypin in the early 20th century, such carriages were used to transport settlers to the East of the country. They were lower than normal passenger ones, and had departments for luggage, poultry and cattle. Later, they were re-fitted and used to transport convicts. Until then, prisoners had to walk or ride horses, and many died in transit.

In the evening, when it got completely dark, a van took us to the train station. Volodarka is situated a few blocks away from the station, so the trip only took about ten minutes. There were with machine guns atilt, dogs straining at their leashes. The head of the convoy made a habitual announcement,

"You are now under the orders of the convoy. You must fully comply. Any disobedience, any extra step back, forward or to the side will be considered an attempt to escape. We will shoot without warning."

On the appropriate command, we took our bags and walked towards the station. We were surrounded by soldiers with their machine guns at the ready. There were armed men with service dogs in the distance. Trained German Shepherds looked at us indifferently and disinterestedly, but you know it only takes one command to turn them into ferocious predators.

A commuter train shot past us without slowing down. You could see figures of free people in its windows. What a joy it would be to be among them! Oh, life.

Suddenly a dim sheaf of lights started to spin in the darkness in front of us. It was a guard making signals with circular movements of his flashlight. One of the dark carriages stopped right in front of us. Soldiers immediately lined up in front of its doors, forming a living corridor that we passed through on command, one by one, to enter the carriage. The shouts of the soldiers and the dogs barking all got mixed up in one giant cacophony. A soldier by the entrance helped me up to get into the carriage. Another one led me along the corridor and into my compartment. I took my place and looked around. The compartment was separated from the corridor by a barred metal door with a large padlock on the other side. The two lower beds were the same as in a regular passenger carriage (despite being wooden), but the top two were a solid board across the whole compartment with a small aperture to let a prisoner climb in. More convicts arrived to fill the compartment. Some of them looked around busily and climbed up to take a "sleeping" seat.

The train slowly started to move and gradually gained speed. I pressed my forehead against the cold, barred door and looked at the corridor. The windows were painted over with yellow paint. In some places the paint was scratched, and you could see trees quickly coming in and out of sight behind the window. The corridor was guarded by soldiers who chatted and laughed when passing each other. It was approaching midnight. Most men in our compartment were sleeping, others were smoking, eating or exchanging a few meaningless phrases. I didn't talk to anyone, deep in my thoughts, despite not being fully aware what I was thinking.

"Where are we, boss?" someone asked the escort during a particularly long stop at one of the stations.

"Orsha, your final stop. Penal Colony No. 8. Come out one by one when I call out your name," the head of the convoy answered.

Penal colony No. 8...

"Alright, convicts," a dorky-looking officer who looked somewhat like Winnie the Pooh, opened the door of the holding cell at 6 a.m. at our new place. "Come out one at a time."

A corridor with tile walls. And then the light. The sun, not electric bulbs. Eyelids involuntarily covered our eyes, trying to protect them from a natural light that we had grown so unaccustomed to over a year and a half of living in cellars.

Flowerbeds placed in brightly colored car tires, a bronze bust of Soviet writer Maksim Gorky, brick buildings constructed in the 1960s and hundreds of people scurrying around carrying spades, brooms and rakes, some wearing red arm bands.

They led us to the store: a sort-of warehouse, where each of us was assigned an aluminum mug, a spoon, a towel, bed linen that had grown yellow from frequent washing, a mattress, a pillow, a blanket, a uniform (black cotton pants and jacket that shrunk two sizes after the first wash), boots and a light-green quilted jacket made from old military trousers.

Then there was the quarantine unit — a separate two-storied building, where everyone that arrived that day was supposed to spend a couple of weeks before being assigned to a unit.

"Listen up, convicts," the short, fat quarantine unit head nicknamed Rollton (a popular brand of cheap instant noodles) decided to give us directions instead of a welcoming speech, "leave your bags here, change into your new uniform and line up for a roll-call."

"What roll-call?" I asked someone.

"To see of everyone's here. In the morning and evening. Four times a day at the quarantine. At the pre-trial detention center they simply count heads, here they call out every single name."

"I could use a nap, boss," someone in the crowd complained.

"You'll have a chance to sleep after the roll-call and breakfast," Rollton replied. "If you sign the papers."

The "papers" turned out to be a "letter of commitment to appropriate behavior".

Divide and conquer is a famous Roman rule. It is every prisoner's personal choice whether to sign the papers or not. Of course, it was the cops who came up with this idea to divide the prisoners into two opposing camps. On the one hand, you can't get an early parole without signing the papers. On the other hand, prisoners who haven't signed them have a higher place in the criminal hierarchy than the ones who did. The men who have signed the papers proudly call themselves "decent". The rest they refer to as "jackasses".

Our days at the quarantine unit were monotonous: hungry, cold and indefinite. Canteen three times a day, moronic lectures on subjects like "Protecting Yourself", "A Man among Men", "The Formula of Human Happiness", "The Meaning of Life". The point of being there was defined best by Captain Rollton, "Your task is to break the facility's rules as little as possible," he said, "And ours is to pretend we've fixed you and give you an early parole."

Assignment to a unit is looked forward to by everyone. What do they have at that unit? — Sewing. What about that one? — Woodwork. Which unit has the most space? I want to go to that one — I've got friends there. In the end, I was assigned to Unit No. 7.

I have to warn you — I'm not going to describe everything I've seen at the colony — it would take more than one book, and I can't write as well as that chronicler of the Soviet Gulag system, Aleksandr Solzhenitsyn. A modern prison camp doesn't look (and I'd like to stress that this concerns looks most of all) much different from the ones seen by writers Shalamov, Dovlatov or Solzhenitsyn. Also, until you find yourself behind the bars, even the most talented description can't make you understand what it is really like. I will, therefore, only tell you what seemed strange to me as a young man who was facing the Soviet prison colony system for the first time.

CHAPTER 61

WHY WORK WHEN YOU DON'T NEED TO?

At the industrial zone of the colony fights break out quite frequently as prisoners try to scramble for enough metal to make $5 a month

In most countries, a prison is the main type of punitive institutions. In Belarus, this title belongs to the penal colony, also known as the zone, or, Soviet-style, as a camp. Today, colonies only exist on the territory of the former Soviet republics, in India and Israel.

Technically, our current penal system is based on Gulag ideology.

Colonies remain as a legacy of the Soviet period, when it was believed a man could be "fixed" or "bettered" through compulsory work. The system (80 to 120 people in a unit) was based on the idea that labor and the influence of the collective were the best means of correctional education. At that time, the colony system was an extension of the Soviet state and a way to access cheap labor.

Today, everything has changed, but prisons remain the same. Officials say that prison labor is no longer used for commercial profit but that's a lie. It is being used, and used a lot. However, there isn't much demand for manual work. Also, the question of prisoners' labor engagement includes a huge contradiction: working prisoners must support themselves financially (but they only receive 25% of the money they earn), while prisoners who don't work are provided for by the state. Thus, you can't help asking yourself, why should I work if I don't need to?

The industrial zone is separated from the living area by a barbed wire fence. There is a woodworking workshop, metalwork manufactory (where they produced 20-litre metal canisters) and a sewing section. In Europe, the state must provide working convicts with the same salaries and working conditions as free people have. Here, you'll be lucky to get $5 a month.

There is a guy called Dan in my section. A drug addict in his early thirties. He was smoking pot in the company of two other guys and passed the joint to the guy on his right, then to the guy on his left. That was enough to be found guilty of drug distribution, § 328.3 of the Criminal Code, and be handed an 8-year sentence. Of course, judges understand that eight years is too harsh for one joint, but they can't help it — their hands are tied by the law — article 328.3 is punishable by eight years at least.

Recycling of nonferrous scrap metal at the colony's metal workshop

Dan spent the last four years working six hours a day making mittens and aprons. He will get out of here in a week. His only relative, his 99-year-old grandmother died four months ago. He hadn't saved up any money over the time spent in the colony. Of course, he will be given about five dollars for the bus ride to the city, but he hasn't got anywhere to go to. No family, no money and no documents. A vicious circle. Now try to guess how long it will take Dan to steal something. The right answer is about two days. On the first day the fear of going back to prison will be too great, but then hunger, a very serious argument, will take its toll and Dan will try to pick someone's pocket. Or nick a bag. And he'll be sent back to jail. Then he'll get out, be caught again, and be sent back. And he will remain a prisoner his entire life: cursing his fate, our government and the justice system.

CHAPTER 62

HIGH-SECURITY PENAL COLONY

Me and my friend at the local zone next to our barracks, 2012

What's a high-security colony? It is a place I can describe in almost every detail imaginable, but you won't understand it until you are there. It is a place where everything is turned upside down and nothing makes sense. Where the most ordinary things (such as pants, boots, chairs and jackets) have impossible nicknames. Where you are only allowed two care packages of up to 30 kg, two small parcels of 2 kg, two long and two short visits from your family per year. It is a place where a guard will think for you, and you must know your place, not speak and follow orders. A place where you have no rights, only duties.

Soviet leaders never managed to build world communism, or even communism in their own country, but they succeeded in creating it within penal colonies. Identical humiliating clothes, humiliatingly low wages, equal lack of rights and total social stability: you'll be fed, clothed and even guarded. Outside of prison you have to think about how to earn a living, where to live and what to wear. That's why most prisoners are afraid of freedom. Freedom scares them. They all ask, "Where shall I go?"

In the colony, movements are predetermined for years to come. It is a well-defined cycle: medical unit — barracks — canteen — the work room. They know the colony world well and don't know the free world at all. That's why when you meet people who don't want to leave prison, it doesn't seem that frustratingly strange. Some people enjoyed living in the USSR, too.

Penal Colony No. 8 is for repeat offenders. Your day begins at 6 a.m. At 7 you have morning roll-call. Then you have breakfast at the canteen. Then you can choose: some go to work, others sleep, some just wander around. There are pull-up bars, parallel bars, illegal iron (self-made dumbbells), the bath house (six taps giving a thin streams of water), books, church services, a TV showing the same movies and idiotic music videos over and over. The day finishes at 10 p.m.

Every barracks is divided into sections — there are the bedrooms and the Lenin room, which has a TV, a cold-water washbasin (in Belarussian colonies hot water usage is strictly regulated; you are allowed to use the bath house once a week and heating up water and using it to wash your face is a violation of rules which can even get you a spell in solitary confinement). Then there is the toilet, a storage room and an office for the head of the unit. In the bedroom, there are bunk beds, sometimes even triple bunk beds.

You can only walk alone through the colony if you have a special permit. But with enough determination it isn't hard to get around.

There is also the club, the canteen, the bath house, the hospital, the library, the evening school, the administrative office and the church. The whole area is surrounded with two strips of earth that will show footprints if stepped on, barbed wire, a wooden fence and watchtowers with machine gunners.

Everyday things that were completely normal at home here hold a particular significance due to their scarcity. The colony has its own material and moral values. A head of cabbage here evokes the same delight as an exquisite restaurant dish, and having a new tracksuit makes you feel like a millionaire. Due to shortages, most ordinary objects are considered luxury. Knitted sweaters and polo T-shirts are forbidden — you can only have collarless shirts. You can't untie the flaps on a flap hat or pull up the collar of your quilted jacket (which defeats the purpose of both objects). Other banned objects are: washing up liquid, shower gel, facewash, deodorants and even toothpicks. You are allowed to have 'tooth powder', which I haven't seen in any store for past twenty years. Any awkward questions will be answered with "that's against the rules".

We aren't allowed to own pornographic magazines or anything remotely similar. Playboy is considered pornographic. As are FHM, XXL, Maxim and even Men's Health.

If it wasn't for TVs, DVD players and banned mobile phones I would have never believed I was living in the 21st century.

CHAPTER 63

AFTER DINNER COMES THE RECKONING

The hospital is located in the same building as the quarantine unit. Doctor's offices, examination rooms, the lab, the operating theatre and a few wards. Unfortunately, it is located on the third floor and elderly people (there is a unit for old and disabled prisoners; we call them Vikings) often have problems getting up there.

We get three meals a day: breakfast, lunch and dinner. According to older convicts, we shouldn't complain: ten years ago prisoners used to get half what we get now. For breakfast, we have porridge. For lunch, we get flavorless soup made from water and a little bit of beetroot and cabbage (never any potato) and dark pasta with bits of pork or chicken skin, potato mixed with pickled cabbage or green peas mixed with barley. I don't get why they can't give us green peas today and barley tomorrow — why they have to mix it all together, like they are feeding pigs.

All three courses are eaten from the same aluminum bowl and there is no way to wash it in between courses. The same with our hands. At least they steam-cook food here: it doesn't come out very tasty, but at least it meets minimal sanitary standards.

For dinner we get boiled potatoes, cabbage and the same porridge as at breakfast. Sometimes we get boiled fish. The closest thing to meat we have is its smell — the kitchen is run by convicts, and they simply steal and sell it. About 700 grams of chicken will cost you two packs of cigarettes. But it is hard to find such a deal. Because at the colony some people are too envious to simply let others be. So, if you manage to find a way of getting something — keep your mouth shut. If your neighbors find out, you'll regret it.

However, cigarettes will get you anything. From milk (ten cigarettes per liter) to a cell phone. Winston cigarettes are standard currency. A bucket of potatoes costs four packs of Winston, a month of special food (half a loaf of bread, butter and 650 grams of milk every day) costs twelve packs. Such food is sold by people who get it for medical reasons.

You can use the beetroot salad sold at the local store to make nice enough borsch. Just add a couple of potatoes, fry the salad with onions, and boil it all together on a self-made illegal cooker. We use the fish from the canteen to make cutlets. We use the sweet tea to grow tea fungus. You can use rice mushrooms to make something like weak rice beer.

There are almost no fruit and vegetables, and for some reason they don't give us any sugar. It isn't sold at the store either. The cops say it's to make sure we don't make alcohol. Of course, you can get sugar. It will just cost you $3-5 per kilogram. They don't allow any sugar replacements either. Out of fear of alcohol experiments, they ban honey as well. However, jam and hard candy are sold openly at the store — just add some self-made yeast and put it in a warm place…

You don't need to go to the canteen yourself. Instead, you can pay

$3-5 a month to get someone to bring food to you. These people are disparagingly called horses. Some of them get more money, some less, and some will also wash your dishes for the same pay. Of course, some people work for free — out of fear.

Some food can be bought at the colony store. You can go twice a month, but it won't be easy. It won't be easy because the tiny store (about six square meters) can hold up to thirty people at any one time. Not more than half of them are actual customers, the rest are just curious. The state allows us to spend about $40 a month there. In case you've got a criminal suit or repeated violations of prison rules that sum is reduced to $10. You have to find a way to buy food, tea, cigarettes, toilet paper, pens, envelopes and lots of other things with this money. And the goods are of the lowest quality since prisoners don't have a lot of choice and will buy whatever is available.

Care packages are given out through a small window for about two hours a day. Meanwhile, you can be waiting your turn in -30 degrees. All food is stabbed with a knife, sausage is cut into pieces, cigarettes are carefully examined and the tea is put into see-through plastic bags. They don't allow a lot of the things you can get at the pre-trial detention center: spices, instant porridges, honey, powder milk, mashed potatoes, date plums, pomegranates, grapes, raisins and so on. They will allow some brands of instant soup, but not others. The cops might not mind giving us all we receive in the packages, but their lists of permitted goods haven't changed since the 1980s.

CHAPTER 64

FEMME FATALE

She smells like angels must smell. God, how long I've been waiting for this moment. Maybe not here and not like this, but I've been dreaming about marrying Irina one day.

The high-security prison gives you two long (up to three days) and two short (through a glass and with a telephone) visits a year. If you don't fool around and put some effort into it, you can get four more visits as a reward for good behavior and see your family every two months. To do this, you will have to 'take an active part in the unit's life': draw postcards and posters, play chess and checkers, partake in sports competitions, sing karaoke, recite poems and do something for the colony, such as working in the barracks or the industrial zone.

To see your family costs $20 a day — that's the price of a room at the prison hotel.

"I came to you from a fairy tale," Irina said to me during the official part of our wedding when we exchanged rings (mine didn't fit for some reason, even though at the pre-trial detention center I'd tried on my lawyer's ring and asked them to make mine the same size).

We were now alone in our room.

"Which tale?"

"A good one," Irina gave me her best mischievous smile.

She hasn't changed a bit since the last time I held her in my arms. But now her eyes have grown even dearer to me. God, why is this happening to me? She tells me she lives in hope that I will find a way to get out of here as soon as possible, that she needs me at home, next to her and that she sometimes scolds herself for losing years of life waiting for me — but she can't do anything with herself.

On the first day of the visit your senses are still numb: you don't feel the taste or smell of anything — it will come back to you the next day. And you keep feeling as if you're in a rush: you're constantly afraid you won't have time to speak as much as you'd like and properly enjoy each other before people come and take you away. On the third day, you find out that there was quite enough time. Not for us, the prisoners — but it is hard on our families.

"If I got to prison, I think I would die," Irina said on the third day. "You can't go anywhere, fences are all around, the sky is barred even at the hotel... Also, I'm getting tired of staying in bed."

"Have you brought the book I asked for?" I interrupted. Walled-in by Ivan Mironov."

"Yeh."

"Can I have it?"

"We can use it for some fortune telling."

"How?"

"Easy: you take a book you haven't read, choose a page and line number, open it and read. Sometimes people use the Bible to look for answers. Come on, you first."

"Alright, page 202, second line."

"Babe, do you want to do it three more times?"

"You bet!"

"No, that's what it says in the book. Here, look."

"Doesn't matter, come here…"

The interior design of the prison hotel is very similar to that of student dorms from the 1980s. Two shower rooms that close at 10 p.m. Two Soviet fridges in the kitchen, badly made cast iron kettles, aluminum pans and pots, prehistoric cookers. It's not as hard on us, prisoners, we are used to all sorts of deprivations, but why should our family suffer, when they, free people, come to see us and pay $20 for an opportunity to do so?

The toilets are horrible (it's best I leave them undescribed), all the taps have hot water only, and you'll have to struggle for at least ten minutes to get a somewhat comfortable temperature.

The thirty rooms are tended by just one cleaner, so you can't expect even the lowest standards of cleanliness. There are no dishes in the rooms — you'll have to bring them with you, even mugs and spoons. There are only five rooms with TVs, some of the rest have a radio. Two pieces of purple fabric about 10 cm wide instead of curtains. Worn out squeaky beds, sheets covered with suspicious spots and radiators that are turned off in March.

"Do you know your phone's bugged?" I asked Irina before it was time to leave.

"I know, I've been told. But I don't get, why. They've got you already."

"I guess they want to find my brother. Although I don't see, how — even I don't know where he is. Do you remember the letters Lenin wrote from prison?"

"I don't think I do."

"Right, they had stopped teaching Lenin when you went to school. He wrote with milk that he poured into an inkpot made from bread. When he was caught, he simply ate the inkpot. To read the letters written in milk you have to keep it above a candle. Or press it with an iron. You can use lemon juice instead of milk — it gives the same effect. So, if you ever get an unusual letter from me — press it with an iron."

"This all is so unsettling, Sergey."

Two nights in a row, Irina cried on my shoulder, and I tried to comfort her and promise her that soon everything was going to be alright. But, to be honest, I had tears in my own eyes as well. It would have been easier if I was alone. I would be given a sentence and I would serve it. But now I'm responsible for her future too.

CHAPTER 65

THEIR WAYS

Rumors spread so rapidly, it normally takes about an hour for the whole colony to know. This might be the only place in the world where sound travels faster than light. What do they talk about? About pardons, reduced sentences, about dozens of boring things, about their hopes. They make up things and then they believe in them.

Another thing I have noticed behind bars: people hardly ever listen to each other. Everyone tries to tell his life story and his hopes. Once it's his turn to listen, he starts to zone out.

A particularity of the Belarussian criminal world (in comparison to Russia) is the fact that it almost completely lacks professional criminals — people who make their living completely from illegal activities. All our mob bosses are either dead or steer clear of Belarus. All the remaining professional criminals are safely tucked away in maximum-security prisons. The rest are what we call gentlemen of fortune, the type who steal to drink and then get caught when they get drunk. My friend Baton was right, the criminal world has grown puny. It will take some time for you to learn how to turn people down. Say, a fellow inmate borrows a couple of packs of cigarettes from you. You may think that at a high-security colony people will stand by their words. But they don't, and you may never see your cigarettes again.

Cops here don't stand by their word either. Say, you write a request to the head of the unit (like I did when I wanted to get married to Irina). A few days later you still haven't heard from him, so you ask where your application is. A fat captain swears he's taken it to his boss. However, it turns out he used it as a tablecloth when he was cutting up sausage, and then threw it in the trash.

CHAPTER 66

THE CORRECTIONAL PROCESS

"What are you doing?" Irina once asked me on the phone.

"Drawing a poster."

"Drawing what?!"

"A poster."

"Have you gone mad? A grown man drawing a poster…"

"That's nothing: yesterday I took part in a poetry reciting contest. They gave me a diploma."

"Right. Just like back in the USSR."

"But this is USSR. Everything is like in the 1960s. Posters, activity lists, propaganda. Everything is fake."

"Do you at least have a library?"

"We do, but it's got nothing to read. I'm not interested in Russian classics — I read enough of them at school. Neither do I like bad modern detective novels. The rest of the library is books on Marxism-Leninism."

I recently wrote to the Ministry of Education to ask if I could do a university course from behind bars. It turned out technically I could, but there is "no practical way" it can be done.

The worst thing about the colony is being isolated from the society. And the gradual degradation that entails. Just one year later you'll catch yourself having trouble finding the right words when speaking to someone from outside of jail. The phrases just don't come out as nicely as they used to.

I remember once, before New Year, we were visited by Mikhail Lyukhter, a good man and high-up official. He suggested we buy a few New Year presents to send to the children of some prisoners.

I bought five. I signed notes, put them inside every present and waited for them to be mailed. I waited for a day, then another, then a week. We ended up eating the candies in the cell in the middle of February.

CHAPTER 67

NEW YEAR, NO PHONE

At the beginning of 2011, I was still working on my book. Writing it took significantly more time than I expected. The most difficult thing was expressing your thoughts in a brief, yet clear way, and not forgetting the book is being written for other people to read.

I finally got my own phone, a Nokia N97.

I hid it under a fake board in the windowsill. Of course, you realize that if I had wanted to continue selling dumps, I could just as well have done it from my cell phone. Instead, I kept writing my book. I even tore the page with a list of people who owed me money out of my notepad. Let me remind you how I got sent to jail the second time. When I got out of Volodarka, I didn't plan on returning to carding. But by the time I was released, my former partners and clients owed me about $400,000. Many of them couldn't pay me and asked me to provide them with dumps, so they could make the money to pay me back. So, I gave them dumps and, slowly but surely, got my money back. It didn't take me long to return to carding without even noticing it. It's like smoking: one day you've given it up and haven't smoked for six months, the next day you take a few puffs and you're back in the habit.

In the colony, phones are owned by the people who can afford them. They cost about ten times more than on the outside (starting from about $100 for the most basic model: you can even get an iPhone if you want one) and at our camp about 20% of inmates have one. Some camps have more, some have less.

There are a few ways phones get into jails: they can be "thrown in" (a phone is placed in a coffee tin, the empty space is filled with sealing foam, the tin is tightly wrapped in bubble wrap and duct tape and is tossed over the fence) or "legged in" (smuggled in by the cops or independent contractors working at the industrial zone or prison's evening school). However, it was getting more and more dangerous to own a cell phone. The reason was one man: an overly-ambitious officer who used to work as the head of the colony bakery.

The first time I saw him was in the quarantine: some young, self-centered guard called us over when we were coming back from the canteen and made us march all the way back to the barracks because, according to him, the prison director was watching via camera.

"Who's that clown?" I asked one of the guys.

"Fedonenkov. His nickname's General."

Before Baker (the only way we referred to Fedonenkov), mobiles were never kept further away than the table, but now searches raged day and night.

At the beginning, I got my hands on the Baker's schedule and only made calls when he wasn't working. But, a month later, he started coming more and more often, and no one knew when he was going to be working. It was also around that time we started getting night searches (before we had never had any after 10 p.m.) and some ridiculous fancy dress tricks: in the dark, guards changed into prison robes and quilted jackets and mingled with a group of prisoners on their way back from the dinner. Once they reached the barracks, the guards took off the coats (so that everyone could see the uniform) and went for the guys careless enough to let their phones be seen.

"Where are my notes?" I asked Fedonenkov a couple of days after he took away the materials for my book for no apparent reason.

"At the prison director's office. You can get them from him. If he hasn't thrown them away."

"I'm not going to disturb the prison director, he's a busy man. You took two notepads — I'll write another three. If you take those as well, I won't stop writing. And you can't erase things from my memory."

"Aren't you bored of it yet? It'll only get you in trouble. Why write about the prison camp? By the way, I didn't like the way you talk about me."

"People that want to evade the truth don't usually like it," I replied with a quote from Dovlatov.

"Get lost!" Baker waved his hand at me.

"Why don't you get off my back anyway? Don't write a book! Bring me your phone! I mind my own business, don't bother anyone, I help the colony — I paid for the redecoration of the barracks, bought a mixing desk for the music club, I edit movies for you once in a while, I help the church... Aren't there enough people to target? Go pick on them instead!"

"Who even asked you to help the colony? You're here to serve your sentence. Mixing desk my ass."

"You people are used to getting paid for doing nothing."

"Never mind. Give me your phone."

"What phone? I don't own any phones."

"Well, I've been told you do. Are you doubting my sources?" the Baker was basking in self-admiration.

"I don't doubt you've got great sources," I flattered his vanity a little. "The whole camp is full of your agents."

"I have to do something. Otherwise they'd tell my bosses I'm protecting you. And I wouldn't hesitate to search my own brother if I thought he was going to smuggle a phone into the colony."

I decided not to tell him that if he was so honest he should probably stop taking tea, coffee, chocolate and cigarettes from the inmates. Because, first, he wouldn't listen. And, second, behind bars you need to find an opportunity to compromise with the guards one way or another. Today you give them a bar of chocolate and a pack of cigarettes and tomorrow you are allowed to keep something from your care package that you weren't supposed to. Baker was right about one thing: prisoners will sell each other out left, right and center. There's no sense of unity. People from Azerbaijan, Georgia, Armenia or other national minorities stick together. But when it comes to Belarussians, one quality they never fail to demonstrate is envy: it's bad I don't have a cow, but it's much worse that my neighbor has one. This means you have to hide everything you've got.

"I have to do it, that's how my dad raised me," Baker continued.

"Screw you and your dad!" I thought to myself, and bid him goodbye. Despite the fact there was no-one to rat me out (only three people knew about my phone and all of them used it to call home), a bad feeling never left me from that day.

CHAPTER 68

A GOOD COP IS
A DEAD COP

"Zaborschikov, who's lookout tonight?" I asked about the guy who was supposed to give a loud signal when he saw the guards coming. It doesn't matter if it's raining, snowing, windy or scorching hot — he'll be walking around the barracks like a dog on a leash, and he'll do it for hours.

"Kamenok, the old man who didn't pay off his card debt."

"Oh, that guy... Alexey, can you switch with him so he's lookout in the afternoon? He can't see well, and he'd leave his post to make some tea or something."

"Alright, we'll switch from Monday. Otherwise we'll mess up the pay."

Later that day soldiers who are supposed to guard us, paid us a visit. They drop by often. They drink our tea, eat our sweets, and smoke our cigarettes. In return, they share stories about their average lives. We have quite a bit in common: they speak the same lingo, and listen to the same music. Almost every guard deserves to be put in jail — just like every prisoner could do a guard's job.

An hour later they left. I reached into my hiding place to get the phone and charge the extra battery. Suddenly, I heard another search signal. I hid the phone, covered the hiding place with its lid and tried my best to look casual. Unfortunately, I left the screwdriver by the window.

Guards entered, and I offered them tea. They refused and remained sat at the table: not talking, just exchanging looks. Not understanding, what was going on, I looked at Makar, my neighbor, a 23-year-old village guy who had sold a bag of wild cannabis to an undercover cop and got eight years of jail time. I could see the same puzzlement and confusion about what was going on.

Suddenly, I realized they were going to search us. I grabbed the battery that was charging and opened the door to run out of the room.

At the same moment, the lookout guy gave five calls, which was the signal for the prison director, or a search brigade.

I hesitated. Something clicked in my brain, and I started rushing around the room. That's how they got me — Baker and a huge guard who resembled a U.S. Marine — with my hand still clutching the battery.

They found the screwdriver. It took them twenty minutes to figure out how to open it, but eventually they pulled back the curtains and got the phone out of its hiding place. "So much for my Nokia," I thought discontentedly. "It was too good to last long."

"Get dressed, Sergey," said Fedonenkov. "I'll give you something else to write about for your book."

I dressed warmly: thermals, two pairs of warm socks, prison uniform, a scarf, a hat, a quilted jacket, gloves and, accompanied by two guards, I went to the holding cell.

"Well, hello. How did *you* manage to get in trouble?" Major Svistunov, the deputy head of the prison, looked surprised.

"Don't ask."

"Are you going to write an explanatory report?" he inquired.

"What for? I'm not even sure what I'm charged with."

Officially, it's forbidden to have a phone in the colony, so no-one is ever charged with possessing one. Instead, prisoners are accused of violating the rules: not being properly dressed, using unauthorized electronic appliances and so on.

"Let's see." Svistunov opened my papers. "Did not comply with the colony rules and was causing disruption after bed time," he read. "You can write, you didn't comply with the rules because you weren't sleepy."

"That sounds ridiculous."

I refused to write an explanatory report and went to the holding cell, a small room with a concrete bench and no glass in the window frame. I spread the jacket on the bench, took a breath of the crisp, cold air that immediately started to make my nose tingle and finally started to relax. The nervous trembling that was with me for the whole time Baker was present was gradually leaving my body.

The rusty steel door opened with a clank. It was Igor, the most humane guard in the camp.

"There you go, Sergey," he gave me a few more jackets. "Don't want you to freeze to death overnight. It's -24C outside."

Life is a strange thing. For some guards, all the searches are nothing but work that they don't want to go to, while others treat it like playing Cowboys and Indians — they didn't play enough when they were kids, I guess. But for us prisoners it's way more serious than that. For some of us, an illegal phone will mean losing an early release or sacrificing a family visit. And it's all because we want to talk to our families more often than twice a month.

In the morning, I was taken to see Colonel Shulgin, the head of the camp.

"What do you have to say?" the head of the camp gave me a stern look. "Where did you get the phone?"

"I don't want to lie, and I won't tell the truth either," I replied with a phrase I'd prepared in the cell.

"You had a really quality phone: mine is nothing like it. No-one would throw it in, therefore someone must have brought it in. I am very interested in traitors among my staff. I'll give you ten days of solitary confinement to start with. Then the high-security barracks for six months. So, take your time to think about it. When you're ready to talk — ask for an appointment and I'll see you."

We call the head of the prison "boss". The boss is our lord almighty. He's got as much power as the president, even if only over a relatively small number of people. He'll choose whether to punish you or show mercy. In the camp, you don't belong to yourself and that means your life can change at any moment. Everyone is afraid of Shulgin, both prisoners and staff.

Until recently you could get a maximum of fifteen days solitary confinement. Now it's ten. Although, as the guards say, "We don't care if we give you fifteen days twice or ten days three time". We prisoners know the difference.

"Let's have a chat," Baker's curly head appeared in the doorway of the holding cell.

"As you say," I agreed, and we went upstairs to his office.

"Here you go," Baker held out a cup of tea once we were comfortably sat in armchairs. "I made it for you. With sugar."

I took a sip with delight. After being in -24 degrees outside, the warming effect of the tea was as good as that of a good French cognac.

"So, what's the phone's password?" Baker began.

"Are you kidding?"

"I beg your pardon?" Baker didn't sound pleased.

"I once told a cop the password for my computer and was handed ten years in jail. So, let's not start this."

There was nothing illegal in the memory of my Nokia, but I didn't want anyone to look at my unfinished book or my private photos.

"What does that have to do with me?" Baker unbuttoned the collar of his shirt as if it was too tight, and rose a little above the table. "If a cop once screwed you over, doesn't mean we're all like that."

"Right. Bad cops get bad coffins, and good cops — good ones," I remembered an old joke. "You're all the same."

"I see this conversation isn't going to work out."

"I don't think it is."

After lunch, I was taken to solitary confinement.

CHAPTER 69

HUMAN EXHAUSTION

The disciplinary unit is like a prison inside the prison.

The first thing that happens, just like at any other jail, is they make you take off your watch and take away your shoe laces. Then they give you worn out trousers that are so old they are barely knee length and an equally shabby coat with "Disciplinary Unit" written across it. The only personal belongings you're allowed to have in the cell are socks, underwear, thermals, soap, toothbrush, toothpaste, toilet paper and a towel. You're not allowed to have slippers, so for your whole term you'll have to wear your sweaty shoes. Or socks.

"So, hacker, which cell will you go to?" asked Tamtik, the guard in charge of the disciplinary unit.

Most people have only a very vague understanding of what a hacker is. They don't see any difference between a hacker and, say, a carder. In their opinion, a person who breaks into someone's email account and a person who uses the Internet to steal money from people's credit cards, belong to the same trade. These people will call anyone whose crime is even remotely connected with computers a hacker. "Hacker" became my prison nickname very quickly.

"I'll go talk to the guy in No. 8 first."

Cell No. 8 is usually taken by high-ranking criminals who control everything happening in the disciplinary unit and know who are in the other cells. They use a "computer" — a piece of cardboard — to keep track of newcomers and their cell numbers.

"Name, unit, violation," a husky voice asked from behind the door of cell No. 8.

"Hacker, unit 7, a cell phone."

"Where to?"

"To No. 4". I knew that cell had two radiators, which was crucial given the bitter frost outside.

"Why there?"

"I've a reason."

"What reason?"

"Do you want the whole corridor to hear?"

"Alright, go."

Cell No. 4 reminded me of Volodarka. Two by four meters, the same concrete 'fur' on the walls, two light bulbs covered with iron nets, a barred window, a washstand, a toilet, a small cupboard for personal belongings, four plank beds you are only allowed to use during the night, a few metal stools fixed to the concrete floor and a narrow table. Inmates were drying bread on the radiator.

"Hello, come in. What unit you from?" I was invited into the darkness of the cell.

"No 7."

I sat on a bed and started studying the faces of my fellows in misfortune: five men who clearly hadn't shaved for over a week.

"A phone?" asked a huge guy whose face I thought looked familiar.

"Yes," I sighed.

"Us too," the big man smiled. "About half the people got here because of a cell phone. Mosquito," he introduced himself.

In the corner of the cell under the washing stand was an adder — a metal spiral connected to the wiring, which emitted a nice warm glow.

"Until we made it," Mosquito caught the direction of my eyes, "we hadn't slept for three nights and the cell was so cold we could see our breath. By the way, what's the temperature outside?"

"Gets down to -30 degrees at night," I delivered the bad news. "How do I get in touch with my unit? Mother's Day is around the corner and I want to tell the guys to congratulate my girls. It's my first time at the disciplinary unit."

"Your unit is just a few feet away," said one of the guys. "It'll be easier to just shout it over the wall."

"How many people does the cell fit?"

"Four."

"We are six. How are we going to sleep? The beds won't fit everyone."

"On the floor."

"But it's concrete." I shivered at the idea of the inevitable touch of the cold floor.

"This isn't a resort," one of the guys shrugged.

"And there's no fresh air either," I looked at the closed window.

"We keep it open ten minutes a day, it's too cold otherwise."

"What about walks?"

"Fat chance. Have you brought any cigarettes, by the way?"

"No. They took me straight from the unit, I had no chance to get my things. And I don't smoke, I quit."

Smoking isn't a habit, it's an addiction, and the disciplinary unit makes you see it crystal clear. In your search for tobacco you will tear apart cigarette butts, turn pockets inside out, slice insoles open (they are often used to hide tobacco) and shake out shoes. Cigarettes are flattened into thin strips that are hidden in every place imaginable. Alternatively, they are wrapped in tin foil, put into several plastic bags (or a condom) and are smuggled in inserted in one's ass. That's called torpedoing.

According to Solzhenitsyn, a disciplinary unit cell must be a) cold; b) damp; c) dark; d) hungry. The first three are absolutely true, but it was a complete revelation that you get fed much better than the rest of the colony: portions are twice as big, and I finally saw some meat. Drinks, however, are poured into one common bowl as there are no cups.

The light is always on, the windows are closed, and there are no clocks, so you don't really notice day becoming night. At night, we try to sleep on the hard, wooden plank beds (they don't give us any mattresses) and on the floor during the day. The average temperature is around 10 degrees, and that's with our little heating device working constantly. Feeling cold all the time makes you feel sleepy. The time flows as slowly as vodka when you've just taken it out of the freezer and are pouring it into a glass. There's absolutely nothing to do except eating and sleeping.

"Hey, Pavel," I call one of the guards over. "Give me some paper and a pen, would you?"

And that's how I started writing the book again. I was writing at night on bits of wrapping paper (there was no other option) in the dim light of a 15-Watt light bulb. During the day, I did push-ups and squats and washed my clothes in the washbasin.

I celebrated my 28th birthday in the disciplinary unit. Friends from the colony managed to pass me some tea, cigarettes and chocolate. I really wanted some coffee, but I had to make do with what I had.

The disciplinary unit, just like any other institution where people are locked in small spaces, makes the people around you very important. It's filled with the most progressive part of the prison population: almost half of the prisoners were sent here for using phones.

On your last day, there's only one thing you keep wondering about: will they let you go or give you extra days. Additional punishment (ten extra days at the disciplinary unit) can be allocated in three ways: either you are taken to the boss, he comes over, or the guards come over and inform everyone, "Buday, the boss has given you 10 more days, Shevelev, ten for you too, Pavlovich, ten more."

"What for?"

"You were sleeping on the floor," the guard reads the official statement.

"But I wasn't sleeping!" you boil over.

"Well, you understand."

You may be awake in the afternoons (despite the fact cells are usually overcrowded and you need to take turns sleeping), wear uniform at all times, make the cell spotless on the day you're in charge of cleaning, but if someone up there says "get him", there'll always be something you've done wrong. As long as there's a man, there's a crime.

I didn't even notice my second batch of ten days come to an end. If I was given ten more days, I was going to go on hunger strike. Some of my cellmates would smoke PTFE — some plastic crap that significantly raises your body temperature when you inhale its fumes — and were hoping to get taken to hospital, but I don't take kindly to such experiments.

"Isn't it sad, guys?" I grimly addressed my cellmates. "It's the twenty-first century, and the prison is damp and dark. We sleep on the cold floor and tuck toilet paper into cracks in the window frame to conserve heat, we hide pen ink holders in toothpaste, we smoke cigarettes that we have smuggled in our own asses and we eat with shards of aluminum spoons…"

"It used to be worse, we used to have on and off days."

"What do you mean?"

"They would feed us one day and not feed us the other."

"Right."

EPILOGUE

Unfortunately, we don't make rough drafts for life. You can't edit it, leaving out lines you don't like.

A year after our wedding, Irina filed for divorce. She got tired of seeing me as a prisoner obeying someone else's rules. Am I sorry we parted ways? I am — madly sorry. Those were the best days of my life.

In the courtroom they always ask: "Do you admit your guilt? Do you feel remorse?" and you have to say "Yes" if you want to get a shorter sentence. But is that really remorse? It was only after I'd spent four years in prison, which I used to study and examine my life, that I realized why it all had to happen to me: the jail and the failed relationship with Irina. "Just the way a boomerang always comes back," investigator Makarevich once told me, "a crime is inevitably followed with a punishment. The main reason for all crimes in the world, and cyber-crimes in particular, is the illusion of impunity. You may steal for a year, two or five and never get caught. But you will end up in jail. Because not all sentences are given in court…"

I gave carding ten years of my life. The first time I got out of prison not only did I fail to quit, I also started spamming. At the moment, I'm trying my hand at writing. What I will do tomorrow is a mystery. Nobody knows what the future has in store. The only thing I'm sure of is that neither the strictest sentence, nor the prison bosses can change my views — unless I want to change them myself. I've drawn some conclusions, but others remain to be drawn. That's why I remain in jail, and why I still can't get used to it.

There's a heavy smell of cigarettes and fried potatoes, which, thank God, are still available to buy.

The thermometer says it's -2 degrees outside, but the radiators have already been switched off to save money. The radio keeps playing popular prison songs. I get onto my top bunk, take out my notepad and write the last lines of this book. Everything that's in it is true. And all of it will stay with me forever. It's snowing outside. Maybe it's the last snow of the year.

Correctional colony
No. 8, Orsha, Belarus,
March 2012

CHARACTERS MENTIONED IN THE BOOK

Roman Vega (Boa)
One of the founders of CarderPlanet, Ukrainian Roman Vega was arrested in Cyprus in 2003 with Liratto and extradited to the USA. In 2013, he was sentenced to 18 years behind bars by a New York court and is due to be released in 2020. While in prison he has corresponded with lots of people, got to be quite good at yoga and keeps up a prolific blog (www.romanvega.com).

Alexey Stroganov (Flint24)
A moderator at Carder.org and one of the founders of RealPlastic.org, a workshop producing counterfeit credit cards. He was convicted, sentenced to six years in jail and released in 2008.

Gerasim Selivanov (Gabrik)
He was charged with supplying dumps to nearly all the major producers of counterfeit credit cards working in the former Soviet Union. Was on Russia's list of most wanted criminals for years. Finally caught in 2003 and sentenced to 6 years in jail.

Boris Drunkman (Nicron)
He had enough nerve to avoid being arrested in Belarus. Now he is living in Russia, where he is married and raising a child.

Dmitry Golubov (Script)
Arrested in 2005 in Odessa on suspicion of being the founder of CarderPlanet. He spent only six months in pre-trial detention, before

he was released on bail paid by two deputies from the Ukrainian parliament. His case fell apart and he was freed. After his release, he founded and registered the Internet Party of Ukraine. He is married and raising a son. He is currently a deputy in the Ukrainian parliament and a member of the faction backing the current president, Petro Poroshenko.

Ilya Saprykin (Postal)

Found guilty in 2007 of stealing $200,000 from Minsk ATM machines and sentenced to 6 years in jail. Released on amnesty in 2010.

Vladimir Boyankov

Arrested in Minsk in 2007 and charged with the theft of $340,000 in cooperation with police colonels Novik and Miklashevich. He was sentenced to seven years in jail and confiscation of property.

Sergey Novik

A police colonel in Belarus who was arrested in 2007 and charged with abuse of power and creating an organized criminal group, which included Colonel Miklashevich from the same department. According to case materials, the group founded and managed by Novik used counterfeit plastic cards with PIN-codes to steal about $340,000. He was sentenced to eight years in jail.

Andrey Miklashevich

A police colonel in Belarus who was arrested in 2007 and found guilty of abuse of power and sentenced to three years in jail. He was found not guilty two years later. At the moment, he is working in the telecoms industry.

Alexander Makarevich

A police major who investigated cyber-crimes. He was demoted after the 2007 arrest of Miklashevich and Novik. He is currently working at a commercial bank.

Maksim Yastremskiy (Maksik)
A Ukrainian dump seller and a key member of the Albert Gonzalez gang, who was arrested in Turkey in 2007 while at a party at a beach resort. He was found guilty of stealing from Turkish banks in 2009 and sentenced to 30 years in prison. He has twice tried to commit suicide in prison. Eventually, he escaped from prison. Current whereabouts unknown.

Alexander Suvorov (JonnyHell)
An Estonian citizen arrested in Germany in 2008 and extradited to the USA where, along with Gonzalez, he was charged with breaking into computer systems and stealing thousands of credit card numbers, among other crimes. He initially denied all accusations. But in 2011 he admitted selling $10,000 worth of dumps to an American secret agent. Sentenced to 7 years in jail and released in 2014.

Albert Gonzalez (SoupNazi, Segvec)
A U.S. hacker who admitted stealing the details of over 200 million bank cards from the computer networks of major U.S. companies between 2005 and 2007. "I understand it's going to be a long road home," Albert said shortly before the announcement of the verdict. He was sentenced to 20 years behind bars and is due to be released in 2025.

Max Butler (Iceman)
One of the world's most infamous hackers and owner of the CardersMarket forum, the U.S. citizen was arrested in 2007 and three years later sentenced to 13 years in jail for stealing 1.8 million credit cards. He is set to be freed in 2019.

Vladislav Khorokhorin (BadB)

Dubbed "one of world's top five cyber criminals", he was arrested in Nice in 2010 and extradited to the USA two years later. He has dual Ukrainian and Israeli citizenship. He was charged with fraud, illegal accessing to bank accounts and selling confidential information, as well as being one of the founders of CarderPlanet. He was sentenced to 7 years in prison and released in 2017. Since being freed he has said he wants to join the Russian intelligence services.

Sergey Storchak (Fidel)

An administrator of the forum CarderPortal.org, who was arrested in 2010 in New Delhi airport on charges filed against him in the U.S. accusing him of involvement in a cyber-crime ring that stole 40 million credit card numbers. At some point, he escaped from prison in India. His current whereabouts is unknown.

Dmitry Burak (Graph)

My brother. Wanted in the U.S. on charges of selling stolen credit card information on DumpsMarket.

Ryan Knisley (Sonelao)

From at least 2006 he has been a U.S. Secret Service agent. Posing as a dumps buyer, he infiltrates carding circles and makes controlled buys that become the base for felony charges. Was involved in the arrests of Maksik, JonnyHell, Fidel, BadB and me.

Kirill Kalashnikov (Kaizer)

No known information on his whereabouts.

Igor Liratto

A Ukrainian arrested in 2003 along with Roman Vega in Cyprus. He was in prison for about two years before being released.

Pavel Voropayev
No known information on his whereabouts.

Stepan Batyuk
No known information on his whereabouts, although I bumped into him in Minsk in 2007. He was working as a taxi driver.

ACKNOWLEDGEMENTS

It took me over three years to write this book. I received immense support from my mother, my friends Sasha Soroka, Valentin Syulzhin and Tanya Anjukova. I'm endlessly grateful to them and would like to extend special thanks to Lyudmilia Kazakevich, my mother-in-law, for her letters that provided consolation in jail. Also to my brother, Dmitry, for silent approval of all my undertakings and to my best friend Nikolay — no-one has done more for me than he has.

I would like to thank Alexey Kuzmenkov (www.mastak.by) for working on the design of the book, Irina Rebus for the courtroom sketches and other amazing illustrations, my university friend Vadim Shmygov for helping me collect materials for the book as well as giving me the optimism to go on. Thanks to Sergey Zhukov, Boa, BigBuyer, BuyMicro, Sergey Anime and SecurityLab.ru and Pritchi.ru portals.

I would like to acknowledge to the editorial staff of Russian Forbes magazine for the inspiring ideas I often found in their articles, Kim Zetter, a columnist at Wired, Yelena Ankudo, a correspondent at Belgazeta, Kevin Poulsen, the author of the amazing *Kingpin*, and writer Robert Greene, whose books, *48 Laws of Power* and *33 Strategies of War*, helped me to believe in myself.

I would like to thank Vova Maglysh, Sergey Bagautdinov, Igor Barabanov, Arthur Kovalevsky, Igor Barkun, Pavel Gorbatovsky, Vitaly Varlamov, Stepan Shevelev, Valentin Abramov and Vova Kapustin — my buddies of necessity, and tireless listeners. My gratitude goes out to everyone who has read the book, either whole or in part, and gave their recommendations.

Another person I appreciate immensely is Olga Semernaya, who typed out the entire text of the book. Also, my friends Maksim Kostyushko and Katya Kibalchich — they did the best they could to remove everything boring or excessive while still trying to keep the book as my own work.

Julia Kostyushko has always helped me with whatever I asked of her, for which I owe her my deepest gratitude.

Lena Sharova (www.sharovalaw.com) is an amazing American lawyer who provided valuable professional advice in many aspects.

Arkady Bukh (nyccriminallawyer.com), a brilliant criminal defense attorney who has helped many carders and hackers placed in American prisons.

I'm also grateful to my translator, Alexandra Yaroslavtseva, and my colleagues, eNdi, Astal, Liratto and Black Monarch, Dima Naskovets, lawyer Marina Vorobyeva and all the non-indifferent people who, risking their own careers, helped me to work on the book and whose names I unfortunately can't mention for their own safety.

I am grateful to God for allowing me to complete this book and, finally, I would like to thank everyone who believed in me and supported me this whole time. I wouldn't have achieved anything without you.

Made in the USA
Las Vegas, NV
15 November 2021